# The
# Online Dating
# Journal

# The Online Dating Journal

*A comprehensive journal to record your online dating contacts and experiences*

Anita P. Miller

iUniverse, Inc.
New York  Lincoln  Shanghai

The Online Dating Journal
A comprehensive journal to record your online dating contacts and experiences

Copyright © 2005 by Anita P. Miller

iUniverse books may be ordered through booksellers or by contacting:

iUniverse
2021 Pine Lake Road, Suite 100
Lincoln, NE 68512
www.iuniverse.com
1-800-Authors (1-800-288-4677)

For information, contact:
Anita P. Miller
P.O. Box 3457
McDonough, GA 30253

www.theonlinedatingjournal.us
www.todj.us

Book design by Anita P. Miller

first edition October 2005

ISBN-13: 978-0-595-36543-2
ISBN-10: 0-595-36543-4

Printed in the United States of America

For
My mother, Juanita S. Miller, God's greatest creation.
You taught me the meaning of unconditional love. You taught me how to live.
~ I love you. We will meet again. ~

My father, John H. Miller, Sr.
Thank you for being present in my life,
for openly acknowledging your love and always telling me how proud you are of me.
Your love is the beam of support in my life.
~ I love you too. ~

My daughter, Shanáe M. Miller.
While raising you, I prayed for many things. My prayers were answered.
Thank you for being the perfect daughter.
~ My love for you is beyond words. ~

My grandson, Isaiah K. Miller.
You are my gift from God.
~ I love you. ~

# Contents

# Preface—Note to Readers

What an exciting time to be single and dating! Long gone are the days of depending on the matchmaking skills of friends, family, and coworkers. We have given blind dating a complete makeover and called it online dating; it's the ultimate blind date, where you are in control. Online dating is more than a short-lived trend. It's a global phenomenon, and the online dating community continues to grow at a rapid pace.

*The Online Dating Journal* is the necessary online dating accessory that allows you to take dating to the next level.

*The Online Dating Journal* evolved from my personal online dating experiences. When I started dating online, my goal was to find a suitable companion without wasting time. My hectic schedule required me to be efficient yet thorough. Therefore, I tracked members by writing information on random sheets of paper. I then graduated to recording details in notebooks and separating each member's information with Post-it notes. Although my makeshift system proved successful, it needed to be revamped. While researching available online dating tools and tips, to my surprise, I was unable to find any effective online dating tracking tools on the market.

I had marriage on my mind, so I decided to marry my professional instructional design experience to my time management and organization skills: a match made in heaven. The match produced *The Online Dating Journal*. Think about it—tracking members online is no different than managing a project or managing any other essential part of your life. I knew that if the journal helped me streamline my dating efforts, then my forty million online friends would appreciate it as well. The journal's instructional design supports the natural flow of the online dating progression, and the organization ties directly to the time management aspect of the journal.

It contains proven, time-saving mechanisms and allows you to easily identify members. The tracking of correspondence and information can be very important in the event that you forget details or lose contact with a potential mate. If a serious issue ever arises with an online relationship, *The Online Dating Journal*, if used to its fullest capacity, will provide crucial information to help solve the problem.

It is my hope that you enjoy *The Online Dating Journal*, as it also provides fun anecdotes and dating experiences. Do not take them personally or become offended. These are my stories; I just changed the names to hide *my* identity ☺. Dating is recreation and should be an enjoyable experience, so have fun with it. Heck, take some time to even laugh at yourself!

Congratulations on taking full control of your dating rituals. Your potential mate could be just a mouse click away!

# Disclaimer

*The Online Dating Journal* was created to enhance the online dating experience. *The Online Dating Journal* is not a how-to guide to online dating. Every effort has been made to make *The Online Dating Journal* as complete and thorough as possible. However, compiling and completing the member information on the journal pages does not signify that the information the member has given is true or that the member is safe to date. The owner or user of *The Online Dating Journal* is solely responsible for his or her actions and dating experiences. The author or publisher is not responsible for the safety of the journal owner or user, which is based upon his or her dating decisions.

The purpose of this journal is to provide a tracking mechanism to improve the online dating experience. The author or publisher will be neither liable nor responsible to any person or entity with respect to any loss, damage caused, or alleged to have been caused, directly or indirectly, by the information contained in this book.

All names in this book have no existence outside of the imagination of the author and have no relation to anyone bearing the same name or names.

# The
# Online Dating
# Journal

of

# How to Use *The Online Dating Journal*

*The Online Dating Journal* provides a comprehensive way to track members and potential mates you meet online.

Fact: Dating can be exhilarating!

Fact: Dating can lead to connecting with your soul mate!

Fact: Dating can lead to marriage!

Although these are great facts, it is unfortunate that we do not prioritize dating like we do our careers, finances, childcare, and choices in faith. Does dating actually compare to our careers? Absolutely. The key is to make dating a *healthy* priority. Think about your career or an important project. You're focused (making an assumption here ☺), you're aggressive, and you work toward meeting your goals. Then, you meet your goals. Think about how you accomplish your goals: perseverance, organization, and the help of a time management tool. The same methods can be applied to dating; after all, you've already made a significant financial investment when you became a member of the online dating community. Get your money's worth! Remember, it is dating, so you don't have to be as technical as you are in the workplace—and you can add lots of spice. *The Online Dating Journal* is your tool to stay on top of the game of online dating.

*Always remember to maintain a healthy balance.*

Question: Have you ever been in a situation where you have been corresponding with a couple of members online and you could not remember exactly what was communicated, to whom, or when? *The Online Dating Journal* provides areas to journal topics of communication, helping you to avoid confusion and allowing for more meaningful conversations.

Some people might call you a player, but choose to look at it instead as multitasking.

# How to Use *The Online Dating Journal*

The following chapters will help you find compatible matches in an organized manner. Ultimately, tracking members will save you a lot of time. The key is not to be too serious and to always remember to have fun!

**Online Dating Services**—Over time, you may become a member of more than one online dating service and obtain various screen names. Use this section to research online dating services and to track your online service usage.

**Scanning the Globe**—You definitely will spend time scanning through many member profiles listed in the online community. Use this section to track the members you may want to contact at a later date. This section is especially helpful when making final contact selections.

*Example:* It's Monday, and you spied a profile that piqued your interest. You're not sure if you want to make contact. Besides, before you initiate contact, you want to work on your opening line. Just jot down the member's name and information, think about it, and take another look on Thursday. There's no pressure, and the information is available at your fingertips.

**A Trip around the Block**—The good news is that online dating is open to the world's entire adult community. The bad news is that online dating is open to the world's entire adult community. Unfortunately, there may be members who will need to be blocked from contacting you. Use this area to document the details of the blocked member. In the event of a security issue, it will be very important to know the details of any member you have blocked.

**The Online Dating Journey I & II**—Use this area to track your exciting online dating experiences. The journal provides two full pages for each member contact.

**Safety First**—This section contains basic online dating tips. *Read Disclaimer.*

**Your Place** *and Mine?*—Online dating involves a great level of communication that can eventually become a bit routine. Visit this section to find innovative, exciting, and new online date ideas (and, hopefully, record and submit a few of your own).

**Notes**—Private section to further personalize your journal.

Remember the following five simple rules to online dating:

1. Safety First—Trust your instincts, and always use common sense.

2. Shop Around—There's no such thing as love at first click. Don't settle for the first member you track.

3. Have an Open Mind—No one is perfect.

4. Be Yourself—You're beautiful just the way you are. If someone does not accept you for your naturally beautiful qualities, it's their loss. *Enough said.*

5. Enjoy *The Online Dating Journal,* and have fun!

# Online Dating Services

Variety *is* the spice of life. With that being said…

Throughout your online dating journey, it is possible that you will become a member of various online dating services. Regardless of what the little voice in your head is saying, this is perfectly normal. When seeking an online dating service, look at it as shopping for the perfect suit. You know the suit—the one that makes you look and feel like a million bucks. With the popularity of online dating, there are literally thousands of available services. A minor challenge is deciding which online dating services best *suit* your needs.

Niche online dating services are focused on the specific wants and needs of single adults (i.e., Christian singles or singles with disabilities). Looking for a local mate? No problem! There are numerous online dating services specific to location. The world truly is your oyster when it comes to online dating.

> Tip: When searching for specific niches, narrow your search by using an Internet search engine. The more detailed you are in your search, the more successful you will be in a finding the right niche.

When selecting an online dating service, there are core services you will want to research. By knowing the provided services up front, your online dating experiences will be that much more pleasurable. As with any contract, always read the fine print, especially cancellation and billing requirements.

The following checklist serves as a guide when researching the core services of an online dating service provider. The online dating services you select are your decision. Therefore, tailor the checklist to meet your needs.

# Online Dating Services

Name of Online Dating Service_____

| Online Dating Service Checklist |
|---|
| What are the costs and terms of service? *Make sure the cost fits within your entertainment budget.* |
| Is there an auto-renewal policy? If yes, what are the terms of the policy? *If you find love and want to discontinue service, you will need to know the terms of the contract.* |
| Is there a cost to send e-mail messages to other members? *Know what you are getting for your money.* |
| Does the service use a double blind e-mail system? *A very important feature. You do not want someone to receive your personal e-mail address without your permission.* |
| Does the service provide the ability to block members from making contact? If yes, what is the procedure? *This is a crucial feature. You may need to block someone from contacting you. See chapter 5.* |
| Does the service provide instant messaging amongst members? *Great for private chatting when members are logged in at the same time.* |
| Is there an ability to hide your profile while logged in? *Just in case you don't want other members to know that you're online.* |
| Are emoticons available to use when communicating? *These are just plain fun!* |
| Is there an available chat room? Is the chat room private? *Community or one-on-one chatting—what's your pleasure?* |
| Does the service provide "last logged in" details for individual members? *You don't want to send correspondence to a member who has not logged in for a year.* |
| What is the maximum number of pictures that can be posted on the profile? *You will want to know this information prior to your photo shoot. ;-)* |

*With any online dating service, always review the posted safety tips. See chapter 7.*

# Online Dating Services

Name of Online Dating Service_____

| Online Dating Service Checklist |
|---|
| What are the costs and terms of service? *Make sure the cost fits within your entertainment budget.* |
| Is there an auto-renewal policy? If yes, what are the terms of the policy? *If you find love and want to discontinue service, you will need to know the terms of the contract.* |
| Is there a cost to send e-mail messages to other members? *Know what you are getting for your money.* |
| Does the service use a double blind e-mail system? *A very important feature. You do not want someone to receive your personal e-mail address without your permission.* |
| Does the service provide the ability to block members from making contact? If yes, what is the procedure? *This is a crucial feature. You may need to block someone from contacting you. See chapter 5.* |
| Does the service provide instant messaging amongst members? *Great for private chatting when members are logged in at the same time.* |
| Is there an ability to hide your profile while logged in? *Just in case you don't want other members to know that you're online.* |
| Are emoticons available to use when communicating? *These are just plain fun!* |
| Is there an available chat room? Is the chat room private? *Community or one-on-one chatting—what's your pleasure?* |
| Does the service provide "last logged in" details for individual members? *You don't want to send correspondence to a member who has not logged in for a year.* |
| What is the maximum number of pictures that can be posted on the profile? *You will want to know this information prior to your photo shoot. ;-)* |

*With any online dating service, always review the posted safety tips. See chapter 7.*

# Online Dating Services

Name of Online Dating Service_____

| Online Dating Service Checklist |
|---|
| What are the costs and terms of service? *Make sure the cost fits within your entertainment budget.* |
| Is there an auto-renewal policy? If yes, what are the terms of the policy? *If you find love and want to discontinue service, you will need to know the terms of the contract.* |
| Is there a cost to send e-mail messages to other members? *Know what you are getting for your money.* |
| Does the service use a double blind e-mail system? *A very important feature. You do not want someone to receive your personal e-mail address without your permission.* |
| Does the service provide the ability to block members from making contact? If yes, what is the procedure? *This is a crucial feature. You may need to block someone from contacting you. See chapter 5.* |
| Does the service provide instant messaging amongst members? *Great for private chatting when members are logged in at the same time.* |
| Is there an ability to hide your profile while logged in? *Just in case you don't want other members to know that you're online.* |
| Are emoticons available to use when communicating? *These are just plain fun!* |
| Is there an available chat room? Is the chat room private? *Community or one-on-one chatting—what's your pleasure?* |
| Does the service provide "last logged in" details for individual members? *You don't want to send correspondence to a member who has not logged in for a year.* |
| What is the maximum number of pictures that can be posted on the profile? *You will want to know this information prior to your photo shoot. ;-)* |

*With any online dating service, always review the posted safety tips. See chapter 7.*

# Online Dating Services

Name of Online Dating Service_____

| Online Dating Service Checklist |
|---|
| What are the costs and terms of service? *Make sure the cost fits within your entertainment budget.* |
| Is there an auto-renewal policy? If yes, what are the terms of the policy? *If you find love and want to discontinue service, you will need to know the terms of the contract.* |
| Is there a cost to send e-mail messages to other members? *Know what you are getting for your money.* |
| Does the service use a double blind e-mail system? *A very important feature. You do not want someone to receive your personal e-mail address without your permission.* |
| Does the service provide the ability to block members from making contact? If yes, what is the procedure? *This is a crucial feature. You may need to block someone from contacting you. See chapter 5.* |
| Does the service provide instant messaging amongst members? *Great for private chatting when members are logged in at the same time.* |
| Is there an ability to hide your profile while logged in? *Just in case you don't want other members to know that you're online.* |
| Are emoticons available to use when communicating? *These are just plain fun!* |
| Is there an available chat room? Is the chat room private? *Community or one-on-one chatting—what's your pleasure?* |
| Does the service provide "last logged in" details for individual members? *You don't want to send correspondence to a member who has not logged in for a year.* |
| What is the maximum number of pictures that can be posted on the profile? *You will want to know this information prior to your photo shoot. ;-)* |

*With any online dating service, always review the posted safety tips. See chapter 7.*

# Online Dating Services

Name of Online Dating Service_____

| **Online Dating Service Checklist** |
|---|
| What are the costs and terms of service? *Make sure the cost fits within your entertainment budget.* |
| Is there an auto-renewal policy? If yes, what are the terms of the policy? *If you find love and want to discontinue service, you will need to know the terms of the contract.* |
| Is there a cost to send e-mail messages to other members? *Know what you are getting for your money.* |
| Does the service use a double blind e-mail system? *A very important feature. You do not want someone to receive your personal e-mail address without your permission.* |
| Does the service provide the ability to block members from making contact? If yes, what is the procedure? *This is a crucial feature. You may need to block someone from contacting you. See chapter 5.* |
| Does the service provide instant messaging amongst members? *Great for private chatting when members are logged in at the same time.* |
| Is there an ability to hide your profile while logged in? *Just in case you don't want other members to know that you're online.* |
| Are emoticons available to use when communicating? *These are just plain fun!* |
| Is there an available chat room? Is the chat room private? *Community or one-on-one chatting—what's your pleasure?* |
| Does the service provide "last logged in" details for individual members? *You don't want to send correspondence to a member who has not logged in for a year.* |
| What is the maximum number of pictures that can be posted on the profile? *You will want to know this information prior to your photo shoot. ;-)* |

*With any online dating service, always review the posted safety tips. See chapter 7.*

# Online Dating Services

Name of Online Dating Service_____

| Online Dating Service Checklist |
|---|
| What are the costs and terms of service? *Make sure the cost fits within your entertainment budget.* |
| Is there an auto-renewal policy? If yes, what are the terms of the policy? *If you find love and want to discontinue service, you will need to know the terms of the contract.* |
| Is there a cost to send e-mail messages to other members? *Know what you are getting for your money.* |
| Does the service use a double blind e-mail system? *A very important feature. You do not want someone to receive your personal e-mail address without your permission.* |
| Does the service provide the ability to block members from making contact? If yes, what is the procedure? *This is a crucial feature. You may need to block someone from contacting you. See chapter 5.* |
| Does the service provide instant messaging amongst members? *Great for private chatting when members are logged in at the same time.* |
| Is there an ability to hide your profile while logged in? *Just in case you don't want other members to know that you're online.* |
| Are emoticons available to use when communicating? *These are just plain fun!* |
| Is there an available chat room? Is the chat room private? *Community or one-on-one chatting—what's your pleasure?* |
| Does the service provide "last logged in" details for individual members? *You don't want to send correspondence to a member who has not logged in for a year.* |
| What is the maximum number of pictures that can be posted on the profile? *You will want to know this information prior to your photo shoot. ;-)* |

*With any online dating service, always review the posted safety tips. See chapter 7.*

# Online Dating Services

Name of Online Dating Service_____

What are the costs and terms of service? *Make sure the cost fits within your entertainment budget.*

Is there an auto-renewal policy? If yes, what are the terms of the policy? *If you find love and want to discontinue service, you will need to know the terms of the contract.*

Is there a cost to send e-mail messages to other members? *Know what you are getting for your money.*

Does the service use a double blind e-mail system? *A very important feature. You do not want someone to receive your personal e-mail address without your permission.*

Does the service provide the ability to block members from making contact? If yes, what is the procedure? *This is a crucial feature. You may need to block someone from contacting you. See chapter 5.*

Does the service provide instant messaging amongst members? *Great for private chatting when members are logged in at the same time.*

Is there an ability to hide your profile while logged in? *Just in case you don't want other members to know that you're online.*

Are emoticons available to use when communicating? *These are just plain fun!*

Is there an available chat room? Is the chat room private? *Community or one-on-one chatting—what's your pleasure?*

Does the service provide "last logged in" details for individual members? *You don't want to send correspondence to a member who has not logged in for a year.*

What is the maximum number of pictures that can be posted on the profile? *You will want to know this information prior to your photo shoot. ;-)*

*With any online dating service, always review the posted safety tips. See chapter 7.*

# Online Dating Services

Name of Online Dating Service_____

| Online Dating Service Checklist |
| --- |
| What are the costs and terms of service? *Make sure the cost fits within your entertainment budget.* |
| Is there an auto-renewal policy? If yes, what are the terms of the policy? *If you find love and want to discontinue service, you will need to know the terms of the contract.* |
| Is there a cost to send e-mail messages to other members? *Know what you are getting for your money.* |
| Does the service use a double blind e-mail system? *A very important feature. You do not want someone to receive your personal e-mail address without your permission.* |
| Does the service provide the ability to block members from making contact? If yes, what is the procedure? *This is a crucial feature. You may need to block someone from contacting you. See chapter 5.* |
| Does the service provide instant messaging amongst members? *Great for private chatting when members are logged in at the same time.* |
| Is there an ability to hide your profile while logged in? *Just in case you don't want other members to know that you're online.* |
| Are emoticons available to use when communicating? *These are just plain fun!* |
| Is there an available chat room? Is the chat room private? *Community or one-on-one chatting—what's your pleasure?* |
| Does the service provide "last logged in" details for individual members? *You don't want to send correspondence to a member who has not logged in for a year.* |
| What is the maximum number of pictures that can be posted on the profile? *You will want to know this information prior to your photo shoot. ;-)* |

*With any online dating service, always review the posted safety tips. See chapter 7.*

# Online Dating Services

Name of Online Dating Service_____

| Online Dating Service Checklist |
|---|
| What are the costs and terms of service? *Make sure the cost fits within your entertainment budget.* |
| Is there an auto-renewal policy? If yes, what are the terms of the policy? *If you find love and want to discontinue service, you will need to know the terms of the contract.* |
| Is there a cost to send e-mail messages to other members? *Know what you are getting for your money.* |
| Does the service use a double blind e-mail system? *A very important feature. You do not want someone to receive your personal e-mail address without your permission.* |
| Does the service provide the ability to block members from making contact? If yes, what is the procedure? *This is a crucial feature. You may need to block someone from contacting you. See chapter 5.* |
| Does the service provide instant messaging amongst members? *Great for private chatting when members are logged in at the same time.* |
| Is there an ability to hide your profile while logged in? *Just in case you don't want other members to know that you're online.* |
| Are emoticons available to use when communicating? *These are just plain fun!* |
| Is there an available chat room? Is the chat room private? *Community or one-on-one chatting—what's your pleasure?* |
| Does the service provide "last logged in" details for individual members? *You don't want to send correspondence to a member who has not logged in for a year.* |
| What is the maximum number of pictures that can be posted on the profile? *You will want to know this information prior to your photo shoot. ;-)* |

*With any online dating service, always review the posted safety tips. See chapter 7.*

# Online Dating Services

Name of Online Dating Service_____

| Online Dating Service Checklist |
|---|
| What are the costs and terms of service? *Make sure the cost fits within your entertainment budget.* |
| Is there an auto-renewal policy? If yes, what are the terms of the policy? *If you find love and want to discontinue service, you will need to know the terms of the contract.* |
| Is there a cost to send e-mail messages to other members? *Know what you are getting for your money.* |
| Does the service use a double blind e-mail system? *A very important feature. You do not want someone to receive your personal e-mail address without your permission.* |
| Does the service provide the ability to block members from making contact? If yes, what is the procedure? *This is a crucial feature. You may need to block someone from contacting you. See chapter 5.* |
| Does the service provide instant messaging amongst members? *Great for private chatting when members are logged in at the same time.* |
| Is there an ability to hide your profile while logged in? *Just in case you don't want other members to know that you're online.* |
| Are emoticons available to use when communicating? *These are just plain fun!* |
| Is there an available chat room? Is the chat room private? *Community or one-on-one chatting—what's your pleasure?* |
| Does the service provide "last logged in" details for individual members? *You don't want to send correspondence to a member who has not logged in for a year.* |
| What is the maximum number of pictures that can be posted on the profile? *You will want to know this information prior to your photo shoot. ;-)* |

*With any online dating service, always review the posted safety tips. See chapter 7.*

# Online Dating Services

Name of Online Dating Service_____

| **Online Dating Service Checklist** |
|---|
| What are the costs and terms of service? *Make sure the cost fits within your entertainment budget.* |
| Is there an auto-renewal policy? If yes, what are the terms of the policy? *If you find love and want to discontinue service, you will need to know the terms of the contract.* |
| Is there a cost to send e-mail messages to other members? *Know what you are getting for your money.* |
| Does the service use a double blind e-mail system? *A very important feature. You do not want someone to receive your personal e-mail address without your permission.* |
| Does the service provide the ability to block members from making contact? If yes, what is the procedure? *This is a crucial feature. You may need to block someone from contacting you. See chapter 5.* |
| Does the service provide instant messaging amongst members? *Great for private chatting when members are logged in at the same time.* |
| Is there an ability to hide your profile while logged in? *Just in case you don't want other members to know that you're online.* |
| Are emoticons available to use when communicating? *These are just plain fun!* |
| Is there an available chat room? Is the chat room private? *Community or one-on-one chatting—what's your pleasure?* |
| Does the service provide "last logged in" details for individual members? *You don't want to send correspondence to a member who has not logged in for a year.* |
| What is the maximum number of pictures that can be posted on the profile? *You will want to know this information prior to your photo shoot. ;-)* |

*With any online dating service, always review the posted safety tips. See chapter 7.*

# Online Dating Services

You may become a member of various online dating services and may obtain more than one screen name. Use this section to track your online service usage.

Name of Service _____
User/Screen Name _____
Term of Service _____
Fees _____
Web site Address _____
Other _____

Name of Service _____
User/Screen Name _____
Term of Service _____
Fees _____
Web site Address _____
Other _____

Name of Service _____
User/Screen Name _____
Term of Service _____
Fees _____
Web site Address _____
Other _____

Name of Service _____
User/Screen Name _____
Term of Service _____
Fees _____
Web site Address _____
Other _____

# Online Dating Services

You may become a member of various online dating services and may obtain more than one screen name. Use this section to track your online service usage.

Name of Service       _____
User/Screen Name      _____
Term of Service       _____
Fees                  _____
Web site Address      _____
Other                 _____

Name of Service       _____
User/Screen Name      _____
Term of Service       _____
Fees                  _____
Web site Address      _____
Other                 _____

Name of Service       _____
User/Screen Name      _____
Term of Service       _____
Fees                  _____
Web site Address      _____
Other                 _____

Name of Service       _____
User/Screen Name      _____
Term of Service       _____
Fees                  _____
Web site Address      _____
Other                 _____

# Scanning the Globe

**W**hen you enter the world of online dating, it's like being a kid in a candy store. You can almost hear yourself saying, "Blue eyes, brown eyes, and green eyes, *oh my!*" In other words, the number of potential matches is immeasurable and can be a bit overwhelming.

With so many possibilities, and without an effective tracking method, you could literally send e-mails and emoticons to several dozen people. Without timely follow-up, you could miss out on meeting your future mate or even a good friend. *The Online Dating Journal* will save you time. When you receive matches and scan profiles, use the following pages to write down potential contacts—these are the members who you are considering to contact or members who you think are just plain *hot!*

*Don't be like "Moonlighting Morgan," who sent so many correspondences and emoticons that the majority of free time (and part of the workday) was spent corresponding online. Online dating was a part-time job for Morgan. Needless to say, many of the important areas of Morgan's life were neglected. A word to the wise, pace yourself to find the one (or three) who is right for you. Online dating is going to be around for a very long time, so there's no need to rush.*

As you are scanning the globe, ask yourself how much time you have to dedicate to online dating? Remember, it's not only about you. (OK, we know that it really *is* all about you; let's just pretend for a minute that it's not.) If you initiate an online conversation by sending an e-mail or emoticon, be sure that you have time to reciprocate when a member responds to you. The members you contact are looking forward to communicating with you. If you never respond, it's like waiting for the phone call that never comes—you know the feeling. On the flip side, never feel obligated to respond to everyone who comes your way. Some members will contact you directly, others will be forwarded to you by automated matching systems, and members may also be sent to you by your friends. It's your life, your call. No pressure.

I love to scan the globe, and I always approach online dating with a positive attitude. Every time that I'm in the online dating world, I feel that *this* will be the day I find my mate. OK, so it doesn't happen that easily, but I do keep a positive outlook. I operate in three zones when I'm scanning the globe. The zones keep me focused, and I sometimes find myself laughing out loud when using them.

# Scanning the Globe

**T**he **Yummy Zone**—When I see a photo and all I can say is, "Yum," I know that I am in the Yummy Zone. All I can do at that point is remove my hand from the mouse, sit back in my chair, and let my mind run free. These are the photos that make you want to skip the profiles and get on with the ceremony. Sometimes, I just need to step away from the computer. I know that this zone is all about the physical attributes, but, hey, at least I'm honest. Although it's dangerous for *me*, I love the Yummy Zone. For my own good, I don't stay in this zone very long.

**The "Oh My" Zone**—These are the photos and profiles that make me say, "Oh my!" I cannot believe that people would actually expect someone to respond to their sexually explicit profiles or to pictures where they are frowning and their hair is an absolute mess. The "oh my" profiles are the ones that I would never contact; they serve as a reminder for me of what not to do. I look at it as comic relief. Yes, of course, we all have our "oh my" moments, but those moments should be private, not shared with the world. I guess there *is* somebody for everyone. If you don't have anything nice to say, just say, "Oh my!"

**The Comfort Zone**—This by far is my favorite zone. These men are not in the Yummy Zone, and they definitely are not listed as "oh my" men. The initial review of their profiles says that they are perfect companions for me—they're handsome and toting great profiles. These are the ones who are always worth pursuing. It's a great fit and feels good. It's very comfortable here.

As I was creating *The Online Dating Journal,* I did a little scanning on the side; I couldn't help myself. I found a man with a very yummy profile. When I have some downtime, I plan to contact him. This man was yummy from every angle. You see, it's not just about the physical appearance—it's about having a good balance of both elements. My next step is to make contact and then to do my homework. I don't want to jump without a parachute.

Create your own zones (or use mine), and have fun with it. There are some very exciting members just waiting to chat with you!

No, there is not a limit to the number of contacts that you can make. Heck, contact them all if you want—just be prepared for the avalanche of correspondence guaranteed to come your way.

This area is provided for you to track potential contacts. Get in the zone!

# Scanning the Globe Log

*Record your potential contacts.*

Date _____ Screen/Member Name _____ Online Dating Service _____ Other _____
Date _____ Screen/Member Name _____ Online Dating Service _____ Other _____
Date _____ Screen/Member Name _____ Online Dating Service _____ Other _____
Date _____ Screen/Member Name _____ Online Dating Service _____ Other _____
Date _____ Screen/Member Name _____ Online Dating Service _____ Other _____
Date _____ Screen/Member Name _____ Online Dating Service _____ Other _____
Date _____ Screen/Member Name _____ Online Dating Service _____ Other _____
Date _____ Screen/Member Name _____ Online Dating Service _____ Other _____
Date _____ Screen/Member Name _____ Online Dating Service _____ Other _____
Date _____ Screen/Member Name _____ Online Dating Service _____ Other _____
Date _____ Screen/Member Name _____ Online Dating Service _____ Other _____
Date _____ Screen/Member Name _____ Online Dating Service _____ Other _____
Date _____ Screen/Member Name _____ Online Dating Service _____ Other _____
Date _____ Screen/Member Name _____ Online Dating Service _____ Other _____
Date _____ Screen/Member Name _____ Online Dating Service _____ Other _____
Date _____ Screen/Member Name _____ Online Dating Service _____ Other _____
Date _____ Screen/Member Name _____ Online Dating Service _____ Other _____
Date _____ Screen/Member Name _____ Online Dating Service _____ Other _____
Date _____ Screen/Member Name _____ Online Dating Service _____ Other _____
Date _____ Screen/Member Name _____ Online Dating Service _____ Other _____
Date _____ Screen/Member Name _____ Online Dating Service _____ Other _____
Date _____ Screen/Member Name _____ Online Dating Service _____ Other _____
Date _____ Screen/Member Name _____ Online Dating Service _____ Other _____
Date _____ Screen/Member Name _____ Online Dating Service _____ Other _____
Date _____ Screen/Member Name _____ Online Dating Service _____ Other _____
Date _____ Screen/Member Name _____ Online Dating Service _____ Other _____
Date _____ Screen/Member Name _____ Online Dating Service _____ Other _____
Date _____ Screen/Member Name _____ Online Dating Service _____ Other _____
Date _____ Screen/Member Name _____ Online Dating Service _____ Other _____
Date _____ Screen/Member Name _____ Online Dating Service _____ Other _____
Date _____ Screen/Member Name _____ Online Dating Service _____ Other _____
Date _____ Screen/Member Name _____ Online Dating Service _____ Other _____
Date _____ Screen/Member Name _____ Online Dating Service _____ Other _____
Date _____ Screen/Member Name _____ Online Dating Service _____ Other _____

# Scanning the Globe Log

*Record your potential contacts.*

Date _____ Screen/Member Name _____ Online Dating Service _____ Other _____
Date _____ Screen/Member Name _____ Online Dating Service _____ Other _____
Date _____ Screen/Member Name _____ Online Dating Service _____ Other _____
Date _____ Screen/Member Name _____ Online Dating Service _____ Other _____
Date _____ Screen/Member Name _____ Online Dating Service _____ Other _____
Date _____ Screen/Member Name _____ Online Dating Service _____ Other _____
Date _____ Screen/Member Name _____ Online Dating Service _____ Other _____
Date _____ Screen/Member Name _____ Online Dating Service _____ Other _____
Date _____ Screen/Member Name _____ Online Dating Service _____ Other _____
Date _____ Screen/Member Name _____ Online Dating Service _____ Other _____
Date _____ Screen/Member Name _____ Online Dating Service _____ Other _____
Date _____ Screen/Member Name _____ Online Dating Service _____ Other _____
Date _____ Screen/Member Name _____ Online Dating Service _____ Other _____
Date _____ Screen/Member Name _____ Online Dating Service _____ Other _____
Date _____ Screen/Member Name _____ Online Dating Service _____ Other _____
Date _____ Screen/Member Name _____ Online Dating Service _____ Other _____
Date _____ Screen/Member Name _____ Online Dating Service _____ Other _____
Date _____ Screen/Member Name _____ Online Dating Service _____ Other _____
Date _____ Screen/Member Name _____ Online Dating Service _____ Other _____
Date _____ Screen/Member Name _____ Online Dating Service _____ Other _____
Date _____ Screen/Member Name _____ Online Dating Service _____ Other _____
Date _____ Screen/Member Name _____ Online Dating Service _____ Other _____
Date _____ Screen/Member Name _____ Online Dating Service _____ Other _____
Date _____ Screen/Member Name _____ Online Dating Service _____ Other _____
Date _____ Screen/Member Name _____ Online Dating Service _____ Other _____
Date _____ Screen/Member Name _____ Online Dating Service _____ Other _____
Date _____ Screen/Member Name _____ Online Dating Service _____ Other _____
Date _____ Screen/Member Name _____ Online Dating Service _____ Other _____
Date _____ Screen/Member Name _____ Online Dating Service _____ Other _____
Date _____ Screen/Member Name _____ Online Dating Service _____ Other _____
Date _____ Screen/Member Name _____ Online Dating Service _____ Other _____
Date _____ Screen/Member Name _____ Online Dating Service _____ Other _____
Date _____ Screen/Member Name _____ Online Dating Service _____ Other _____
Date _____ Screen/Member Name _____ Online Dating Service _____ Other _____
Date _____ Screen/Member Name _____ Online Dating Service _____ Other _____
Date _____ Screen/Member Name _____ Online Dating Service _____ Other _____

# Scanning the Globe Log

*Record your potential contacts.*

Date _____ Screen/Member Name _____ Online Dating Service _____ Other _____
Date _____ Screen/Member Name _____ Online Dating Service _____ Other _____
Date _____ Screen/Member Name _____ Online Dating Service _____ Other _____
Date _____ Screen/Member Name _____ Online Dating Service _____ Other _____
Date _____ Screen/Member Name _____ Online Dating Service _____ Other _____
Date _____ Screen/Member Name _____ Online Dating Service _____ Other _____
Date _____ Screen/Member Name _____ Online Dating Service _____ Other _____
Date _____ Screen/Member Name _____ Online Dating Service _____ Other _____
Date _____ Screen/Member Name _____ Online Dating Service _____ Other _____
Date _____ Screen/Member Name _____ Online Dating Service _____ Other _____
Date _____ Screen/Member Name _____ Online Dating Service _____ Other _____
Date _____ Screen/Member Name _____ Online Dating Service _____ Other _____
Date _____ Screen/Member Name _____ Online Dating Service _____ Other _____
Date _____ Screen/Member Name _____ Online Dating Service _____ Other _____
Date _____ Screen/Member Name _____ Online Dating Service _____ Other _____
Date _____ Screen/Member Name _____ Online Dating Service _____ Other _____
Date _____ Screen/Member Name _____ Online Dating Service _____ Other _____
Date _____ Screen/Member Name _____ Online Dating Service _____ Other _____
Date _____ Screen/Member Name _____ Online Dating Service _____ Other _____
Date _____ Screen/Member Name _____ Online Dating Service _____ Other _____
Date _____ Screen/Member Name _____ Online Dating Service _____ Other _____
Date _____ Screen/Member Name _____ Online Dating Service _____ Other _____
Date _____ Screen/Member Name _____ Online Dating Service _____ Other _____
Date _____ Screen/Member Name _____ Online Dating Service _____ Other _____
Date _____ Screen/Member Name _____ Online Dating Service _____ Other _____
Date _____ Screen/Member Name _____ Online Dating Service _____ Other _____
Date _____ Screen/Member Name _____ Online Dating Service _____ Other _____
Date _____ Screen/Member Name _____ Online Dating Service _____ Other _____
Date _____ Screen/Member Name _____ Online Dating Service _____ Other _____
Date _____ Screen/Member Name _____ Online Dating Service _____ Other _____
Date _____ Screen/Member Name _____ Online Dating Service _____ Other _____
Date _____ Screen/Member Name _____ Online Dating Service _____ Other _____
Date _____ Screen/Member Name _____ Online Dating Service _____ Other _____

# Scanning the Globe Log

*Record your potential contacts.*

Date _____ Screen/Member Name _____ Online Dating Service _____ Other _____
Date _____ Screen/Member Name _____ Online Dating Service _____ Other _____
Date _____ Screen/Member Name _____ Online Dating Service _____ Other _____
Date _____ Screen/Member Name _____ Online Dating Service _____ Other _____
Date _____ Screen/Member Name _____ Online Dating Service _____ Other _____
Date _____ Screen/Member Name _____ Online Dating Service _____ Other _____
Date _____ Screen/Member Name _____ Online Dating Service _____ Other _____
Date _____ Screen/Member Name _____ Online Dating Service _____ Other _____
Date _____ Screen/Member Name _____ Online Dating Service _____ Other _____
Date _____ Screen/Member Name _____ Online Dating Service _____ Other _____
Date _____ Screen/Member Name _____ Online Dating Service _____ Other _____
Date _____ Screen/Member Name _____ Online Dating Service _____ Other _____
Date _____ Screen/Member Name _____ Online Dating Service _____ Other _____
Date _____ Screen/Member Name _____ Online Dating Service _____ Other _____
Date _____ Screen/Member Name _____ Online Dating Service _____ Other _____
Date _____ Screen/Member Name _____ Online Dating Service _____ Other _____
Date _____ Screen/Member Name _____ Online Dating Service _____ Other _____
Date _____ Screen/Member Name _____ Online Dating Service _____ Other _____
Date _____ Screen/Member Name _____ Online Dating Service _____ Other _____
Date _____ Screen/Member Name _____ Online Dating Service _____ Other _____
Date _____ Screen/Member Name _____ Online Dating Service _____ Other _____
Date _____ Screen/Member Name _____ Online Dating Service _____ Other _____
Date _____ Screen/Member Name _____ Online Dating Service _____ Other _____
Date _____ Screen/Member Name _____ Online Dating Service _____ Other _____
Date _____ Screen/Member Name _____ Online Dating Service _____ Other _____
Date _____ Screen/Member Name _____ Online Dating Service _____ Other _____
Date _____ Screen/Member Name _____ Online Dating Service _____ Other _____
Date _____ Screen/Member Name _____ Online Dating Service _____ Other _____
Date _____ Screen/Member Name _____ Online Dating Service _____ Other _____
Date _____ Screen/Member Name _____ Online Dating Service _____ Other _____
Date _____ Screen/Member Name _____ Online Dating Service _____ Other _____
Date _____ Screen/Member Name _____ Online Dating Service _____ Other _____
Date _____ Screen/Member Name _____ Online Dating Service _____ Other _____
Date _____ Screen/Member Name _____ Online Dating Service _____ Other _____
Date _____ Screen/Member Name _____ Online Dating Service _____ Other _____
Date _____ Screen/Member Name _____ Online Dating Service _____ Other _____
Date _____ Screen/Member Name _____ Online Dating Service _____ Other _____
Date _____ Screen/Member Name _____ Online Dating Service _____ Other _____

# Scanning the Globe Log

*Record your potential contacts.*

Date _____ Screen/Member Name _____ Online Dating Service _____ Other _____
Date _____ Screen/Member Name _____ Online Dating Service _____ Other _____
Date _____ Screen/Member Name _____ Online Dating Service _____ Other _____
Date _____ Screen/Member Name _____ Online Dating Service _____ Other _____
Date _____ Screen/Member Name _____ Online Dating Service _____ Other _____
Date _____ Screen/Member Name _____ Online Dating Service _____ Other _____
Date _____ Screen/Member Name _____ Online Dating Service _____ Other _____
Date _____ Screen/Member Name _____ Online Dating Service _____ Other _____
Date _____ Screen/Member Name _____ Online Dating Service _____ Other _____
Date _____ Screen/Member Name _____ Online Dating Service _____ Other _____
Date _____ Screen/Member Name _____ Online Dating Service _____ Other _____
Date _____ Screen/Member Name _____ Online Dating Service _____ Other _____
Date _____ Screen/Member Name _____ Online Dating Service _____ Other _____
Date _____ Screen/Member Name _____ Online Dating Service _____ Other _____
Date _____ Screen/Member Name _____ Online Dating Service _____ Other _____
Date _____ Screen/Member Name _____ Online Dating Service _____ Other _____
Date _____ Screen/Member Name _____ Online Dating Service _____ Other _____
Date _____ Screen/Member Name _____ Online Dating Service _____ Other _____
Date _____ Screen/Member Name _____ Online Dating Service _____ Other _____
Date _____ Screen/Member Name _____ Online Dating Service _____ Other _____
Date _____ Screen/Member Name _____ Online Dating Service _____ Other _____
Date _____ Screen/Member Name _____ Online Dating Service _____ Other _____
Date _____ Screen/Member Name _____ Online Dating Service _____ Other _____
Date _____ Screen/Member Name _____ Online Dating Service _____ Other _____
Date _____ Screen/Member Name _____ Online Dating Service _____ Other _____
Date _____ Screen/Member Name _____ Online Dating Service _____ Other _____
Date _____ Screen/Member Name _____ Online Dating Service _____ Other _____
Date _____ Screen/Member Name _____ Online Dating Service _____ Other _____
Date _____ Screen/Member Name _____ Online Dating Service _____ Other _____
Date _____ Screen/Member Name _____ Online Dating Service _____ Other _____
Date _____ Screen/Member Name _____ Online Dating Service _____ Other _____
Date _____ Screen/Member Name _____ Online Dating Service _____ Other _____
Date _____ Screen/Member Name _____ Online Dating Service _____ Other _____
Date _____ Screen/Member Name _____ Online Dating Service _____ Other _____
Date _____ Screen/Member Name _____ Online Dating Service _____ Other _____

# Scanning the Globe Log

*Record your potential contacts.*

Date _____ Screen/Member Name _____ Online Dating Service _____ Other _____

Date _____ Screen/Member Name _____ Online Dating Service _____ Other _____

Date _____ Screen/Member Name _____ Online Dating Service _____ Other _____

Date _____ Screen/Member Name _____ Online Dating Service _____ Other _____

Date _____ Screen/Member Name _____ Online Dating Service _____ Other _____

Date _____ Screen/Member Name _____ Online Dating Service _____ Other _____

Date _____ Screen/Member Name _____ Online Dating Service _____ Other _____

Date _____ Screen/Member Name _____ Online Dating Service _____ Other _____

Date _____ Screen/Member Name _____ Online Dating Service _____ Other _____

Date _____ Screen/Member Name _____ Online Dating Service _____ Other _____

Date _____ Screen/Member Name _____ Online Dating Service _____ Other _____

Date _____ Screen/Member Name _____ Online Dating Service _____ Other _____

Date _____ Screen/Member Name _____ Online Dating Service _____ Other _____

Date _____ Screen/Member Name _____ Online Dating Service _____ Other _____

Date _____ Screen/Member Name _____ Online Dating Service _____ Other _____

Date _____ Screen/Member Name _____ Online Dating Service _____ Other _____

Date _____ Screen/Member Name _____ Online Dating Service _____ Other _____

Date _____ Screen/Member Name _____ Online Dating Service _____ Other _____

Date _____ Screen/Member Name _____ Online Dating Service _____ Other _____

Date _____ Screen/Member Name _____ Online Dating Service _____ Other _____

Date _____ Screen/Member Name _____ Online Dating Service _____ Other _____

Date _____ Screen/Member Name _____ Online Dating Service _____ Other _____

Date _____ Screen/Member Name _____ Online Dating Service _____ Other _____

Date _____ Screen/Member Name _____ Online Dating Service _____ Other _____

Date _____ Screen/Member Name _____ Online Dating Service _____ Other _____

Date _____ Screen/Member Name _____ Online Dating Service _____ Other _____

Date _____ Screen/Member Name _____ Online Dating Service _____ Other _____

Date _____ Screen/Member Name _____ Online Dating Service _____ Other _____

Date _____ Screen/Member Name _____ Online Dating Service _____ Other _____

Date _____ Screen/Member Name _____ Online Dating Service _____ Other _____

Date _____ Screen/Member Name _____ Online Dating Service _____ Other _____

Date _____ Screen/Member Name _____ Online Dating Service _____ Other _____

Date _____ Screen/Member Name _____ Online Dating Service _____ Other _____

Date _____ Screen/Member Name _____ Online Dating Service _____ Other _____

Date _____ Screen/Member Name _____ Online Dating Service _____ Other _____

Date _____ Screen/Member Name _____ Online Dating Service _____ Other _____

# Scanning the Globe Log

*Record your potential contacts.*

Date _____ Screen/Member Name _____ Online Dating Service _____ Other _____
Date _____ Screen/Member Name _____ Online Dating Service _____ Other _____
Date _____ Screen/Member Name _____ Online Dating Service _____ Other _____
Date _____ Screen/Member Name _____ Online Dating Service _____ Other _____
Date _____ Screen/Member Name _____ Online Dating Service _____ Other _____
Date _____ Screen/Member Name _____ Online Dating Service _____ Other _____
Date _____ Screen/Member Name _____ Online Dating Service _____ Other _____
Date _____ Screen/Member Name _____ Online Dating Service _____ Other _____
Date _____ Screen/Member Name _____ Online Dating Service _____ Other _____
Date _____ Screen/Member Name _____ Online Dating Service _____ Other _____
Date _____ Screen/Member Name _____ Online Dating Service _____ Other _____
Date _____ Screen/Member Name _____ Online Dating Service _____ Other _____
Date _____ Screen/Member Name _____ Online Dating Service _____ Other _____
Date _____ Screen/Member Name _____ Online Dating Service _____ Other _____
Date _____ Screen/Member Name _____ Online Dating Service _____ Other _____
Date _____ Screen/Member Name _____ Online Dating Service _____ Other _____
Date _____ Screen/Member Name _____ Online Dating Service _____ Other _____
Date _____ Screen/Member Name _____ Online Dating Service _____ Other _____
Date _____ Screen/Member Name _____ Online Dating Service _____ Other _____
Date _____ Screen/Member Name _____ Online Dating Service _____ Other _____
Date _____ Screen/Member Name _____ Online Dating Service _____ Other _____
Date _____ Screen/Member Name _____ Online Dating Service _____ Other _____
Date _____ Screen/Member Name _____ Online Dating Service _____ Other _____
Date _____ Screen/Member Name _____ Online Dating Service _____ Other _____
Date _____ Screen/Member Name _____ Online Dating Service _____ Other _____
Date _____ Screen/Member Name _____ Online Dating Service _____ Other _____
Date _____ Screen/Member Name _____ Online Dating Service _____ Other _____
Date _____ Screen/Member Name _____ Online Dating Service _____ Other _____
Date _____ Screen/Member Name _____ Online Dating Service _____ Other _____
Date _____ Screen/Member Name _____ Online Dating Service _____ Other _____
Date _____ Screen/Member Name _____ Online Dating Service _____ Other _____
Date _____ Screen/Member Name _____ Online Dating Service _____ Other _____
Date _____ Screen/Member Name _____ Online Dating Service _____ Other _____

# Scanning the Globe Log

*Record your potential contacts.*

Date _____ Screen/Member Name _____ Online Dating Service _____ Other _____
Date _____ Screen/Member Name _____ Online Dating Service _____ Other _____
Date _____ Screen/Member Name _____ Online Dating Service _____ Other _____
Date _____ Screen/Member Name _____ Online Dating Service _____ Other _____
Date _____ Screen/Member Name _____ Online Dating Service _____ Other _____
Date _____ Screen/Member Name _____ Online Dating Service _____ Other _____
Date _____ Screen/Member Name _____ Online Dating Service _____ Other _____
Date _____ Screen/Member Name _____ Online Dating Service _____ Other _____
Date _____ Screen/Member Name _____ Online Dating Service _____ Other _____
Date _____ Screen/Member Name _____ Online Dating Service _____ Other _____
Date _____ Screen/Member Name _____ Online Dating Service _____ Other _____
Date _____ Screen/Member Name _____ Online Dating Service _____ Other _____
Date _____ Screen/Member Name _____ Online Dating Service _____ Other _____
Date _____ Screen/Member Name _____ Online Dating Service _____ Other _____
Date _____ Screen/Member Name _____ Online Dating Service _____ Other _____
Date _____ Screen/Member Name _____ Online Dating Service _____ Other _____
Date _____ Screen/Member Name _____ Online Dating Service _____ Other _____
Date _____ Screen/Member Name _____ Online Dating Service _____ Other _____
Date _____ Screen/Member Name _____ Online Dating Service _____ Other _____
Date _____ Screen/Member Name _____ Online Dating Service _____ Other _____
Date _____ Screen/Member Name _____ Online Dating Service _____ Other _____
Date _____ Screen/Member Name _____ Online Dating Service _____ Other _____
Date _____ Screen/Member Name _____ Online Dating Service _____ Other _____
Date _____ Screen/Member Name _____ Online Dating Service _____ Other _____
Date _____ Screen/Member Name _____ Online Dating Service _____ Other _____
Date _____ Screen/Member Name _____ Online Dating Service _____ Other _____
Date _____ Screen/Member Name _____ Online Dating Service _____ Other _____
Date _____ Screen/Member Name _____ Online Dating Service _____ Other _____
Date _____ Screen/Member Name _____ Online Dating Service _____ Other _____
Date _____ Screen/Member Name _____ Online Dating Service _____ Other _____
Date _____ Screen/Member Name _____ Online Dating Service _____ Other _____
Date _____ Screen/Member Name _____ Online Dating Service _____ Other _____
Date _____ Screen/Member Name _____ Online Dating Service _____ Other _____
Date _____ Screen/Member Name _____ Online Dating Service _____ Other _____

# Scanning the Globe Log

*Record your potential contacts.*

Date _____ Screen/Member Name _____ Online Dating Service _____ Other _____
Date _____ Screen/Member Name _____ Online Dating Service _____ Other _____
Date _____ Screen/Member Name _____ Online Dating Service _____ Other _____
Date _____ Screen/Member Name _____ Online Dating Service _____ Other _____
Date _____ Screen/Member Name _____ Online Dating Service _____ Other _____
Date _____ Screen/Member Name _____ Online Dating Service _____ Other _____
Date _____ Screen/Member Name _____ Online Dating Service _____ Other _____
Date _____ Screen/Member Name _____ Online Dating Service _____ Other _____
Date _____ Screen/Member Name _____ Online Dating Service _____ Other _____
Date _____ Screen/Member Name _____ Online Dating Service _____ Other _____
Date _____ Screen/Member Name _____ Online Dating Service _____ Other _____
Date _____ Screen/Member Name _____ Online Dating Service _____ Other _____
Date _____ Screen/Member Name _____ Online Dating Service _____ Other _____
Date _____ Screen/Member Name _____ Online Dating Service _____ Other _____
Date _____ Screen/Member Name _____ Online Dating Service _____ Other _____
Date _____ Screen/Member Name _____ Online Dating Service _____ Other _____
Date _____ Screen/Member Name _____ Online Dating Service _____ Other _____
Date _____ Screen/Member Name _____ Online Dating Service _____ Other _____
Date _____ Screen/Member Name _____ Online Dating Service _____ Other _____
Date _____ Screen/Member Name _____ Online Dating Service _____ Other _____
Date _____ Screen/Member Name _____ Online Dating Service _____ Other _____
Date _____ Screen/Member Name _____ Online Dating Service _____ Other _____
Date _____ Screen/Member Name _____ Online Dating Service _____ Other _____
Date _____ Screen/Member Name _____ Online Dating Service _____ Other _____
Date _____ Screen/Member Name _____ Online Dating Service _____ Other _____
Date _____ Screen/Member Name _____ Online Dating Service _____ Other _____
Date _____ Screen/Member Name _____ Online Dating Service _____ Other _____
Date _____ Screen/Member Name _____ Online Dating Service _____ Other _____
Date _____ Screen/Member Name _____ Online Dating Service _____ Other _____
Date _____ Screen/Member Name _____ Online Dating Service _____ Other _____
Date _____ Screen/Member Name _____ Online Dating Service _____ Other _____
Date _____ Screen/Member Name _____ Online Dating Service _____ Other _____
Date _____ Screen/Member Name _____ Online Dating Service _____ Other _____
Date _____ Screen/Member Name _____ Online Dating Service _____ Other _____
Date _____ Screen/Member Name _____ Online Dating Service _____ Other _____

# Scanning the Globe Log

*Record your potential contacts.*

Date _____ Screen/Member Name _____ Online Dating Service _____ Other _____

Date _____ Screen/Member Name _____ Online Dating Service _____ Other _____

Date _____ Screen/Member Name _____ Online Dating Service _____ Other _____

Date _____ Screen/Member Name _____ Online Dating Service _____ Other _____

Date _____ Screen/Member Name _____ Online Dating Service _____ Other _____

Date _____ Screen/Member Name _____ Online Dating Service _____ Other _____

Date _____ Screen/Member Name _____ Online Dating Service _____ Other _____

Date _____ Screen/Member Name _____ Online Dating Service _____ Other _____

Date _____ Screen/Member Name _____ Online Dating Service _____ Other _____

Date _____ Screen/Member Name _____ Online Dating Service _____ Other _____

Date _____ Screen/Member Name _____ Online Dating Service _____ Other _____

Date _____ Screen/Member Name _____ Online Dating Service _____ Other _____

Date _____ Screen/Member Name _____ Online Dating Service _____ Other _____

Date _____ Screen/Member Name _____ Online Dating Service _____ Other _____

Date _____ Screen/Member Name _____ Online Dating Service _____ Other _____

Date _____ Screen/Member Name _____ Online Dating Service _____ Other _____

Date _____ Screen/Member Name _____ Online Dating Service _____ Other _____

Date _____ Screen/Member Name _____ Online Dating Service _____ Other _____

Date _____ Screen/Member Name _____ Online Dating Service _____ Other _____

Date _____ Screen/Member Name _____ Online Dating Service _____ Other _____

Date _____ Screen/Member Name _____ Online Dating Service _____ Other _____

Date _____ Screen/Member Name _____ Online Dating Service _____ Other _____

Date _____ Screen/Member Name _____ Online Dating Service _____ Other _____

Date _____ Screen/Member Name _____ Online Dating Service _____ Other _____

Date _____ Screen/Member Name _____ Online Dating Service _____ Other _____

Date _____ Screen/Member Name _____ Online Dating Service _____ Other _____

Date _____ Screen/Member Name _____ Online Dating Service _____ Other _____

Date _____ Screen/Member Name _____ Online Dating Service _____ Other _____

Date _____ Screen/Member Name _____ Online Dating Service _____ Other _____

Date _____ Screen/Member Name _____ Online Dating Service _____ Other _____

Date _____ Screen/Member Name _____ Online Dating Service _____ Other _____

Date _____ Screen/Member Name _____ Online Dating Service _____ Other _____

Date _____ Screen/Member Name _____ Online Dating Service _____ Other _____

Date _____ Screen/Member Name _____ Online Dating Service _____ Other _____

Date _____ Screen/Member Name _____ Online Dating Service _____ Other _____

# Scanning the Globe Log

*Record your potential contacts.*

Date _____ Screen/Member Name _____ Online Dating Service _____ Other _____
Date _____ Screen/Member Name _____ Online Dating Service _____ Other _____
Date _____ Screen/Member Name _____ Online Dating Service _____ Other _____
Date _____ Screen/Member Name _____ Online Dating Service _____ Other _____
Date _____ Screen/Member Name _____ Online Dating Service _____ Other _____
Date _____ Screen/Member Name _____ Online Dating Service _____ Other _____
Date _____ Screen/Member Name _____ Online Dating Service _____ Other _____
Date _____ Screen/Member Name _____ Online Dating Service _____ Other _____
Date _____ Screen/Member Name _____ Online Dating Service _____ Other _____
Date _____ Screen/Member Name _____ Online Dating Service _____ Other _____
Date _____ Screen/Member Name _____ Online Dating Service _____ Other _____
Date _____ Screen/Member Name _____ Online Dating Service _____ Other _____
Date _____ Screen/Member Name _____ Online Dating Service _____ Other _____
Date _____ Screen/Member Name _____ Online Dating Service _____ Other _____
Date _____ Screen/Member Name _____ Online Dating Service _____ Other _____
Date _____ Screen/Member Name _____ Online Dating Service _____ Other _____
Date _____ Screen/Member Name _____ Online Dating Service _____ Other _____
Date _____ Screen/Member Name _____ Online Dating Service _____ Other _____
Date _____ Screen/Member Name _____ Online Dating Service _____ Other _____
Date _____ Screen/Member Name _____ Online Dating Service _____ Other _____
Date _____ Screen/Member Name _____ Online Dating Service _____ Other _____
Date _____ Screen/Member Name _____ Online Dating Service _____ Other _____
Date _____ Screen/Member Name _____ Online Dating Service _____ Other _____
Date _____ Screen/Member Name _____ Online Dating Service _____ Other _____
Date _____ Screen/Member Name _____ Online Dating Service _____ Other _____
Date _____ Screen/Member Name _____ Online Dating Service _____ Other _____
Date _____ Screen/Member Name _____ Online Dating Service _____ Other _____
Date _____ Screen/Member Name _____ Online Dating Service _____ Other _____
Date _____ Screen/Member Name _____ Online Dating Service _____ Other _____
Date _____ Screen/Member Name _____ Online Dating Service _____ Other _____
Date _____ Screen/Member Name _____ Online Dating Service _____ Other _____
Date _____ Screen/Member Name _____ Online Dating Service _____ Other _____
Date _____ Screen/Member Name _____ Online Dating Service _____ Other _____

# A Trip around the Block

Once you begin communicating through the dating service's e-mail system or your personal e-mail system, there may come a time when you will have to block a member or two from contacting you. It may be an overzealous member claiming to be in love with you, a member with a vocabulary limited to words of profanity, or, even worse, someone who thinks that sending you sexually explicit materials will move him or her to the top of your dating list. Yes, it sounds unimaginable, but unfortunately, it's reality.

There are many reasons to block a member from sending communications to you. You will have to determine the reason, and you do not have to justify your reasoning to anyone. If a member appears aggressive, dangerous, or just plain creepy, you should block or ignore them. You be the judge.

Each online dating service has its own process of blocking or reporting any unwanted correspondence. You will need to use the method indicated by the individual dating service. You should also note that once you give your personal information (e-mail address) to a member, the dating service cannot control correspondence. At this point, the block will need to be placed through your Internet service provider, provided that your ISP offers e-mail blocking features.

Some people have personal shoppers. I had a personal stalker, *had* being the operative word. Here's my story:

It was a dark and stormy night (really, it was) when I first responded to Mike's inquiry. The e-mail conversations were great during week one. Mike was very charming and interesting. We had corresponded for about two weeks before the online stalking began. With my laptop being my true love, I am often connected, checking e-mail messages, and searching the Web. Therefore, I usually turn around e-mails swiftly—and not as an act of desperation. Admittedly, the trading of e-mails with Mike was speedy. At some point in the communication, he provided a photo; I thought it was fitting to do the same. Once I submitted my photo, Mike ventured to the point of no return: he lost his mind. The next e-mail message that I received from him asked when I could fly into his city. *Me* fly into *his* city? OK, that's another issue that Mike seemed to have, but I digress.

I was in Mike's Yummy Zone, full throttle. He took one look at my picture and had to have me in his arms ASAP. My initial thought was just to tell him to slow it down a bit. However, I didn't want to let him go because he was in my Comfort Zone. He was very charming, and, initially, we had chemistry. And then it happened—eight e-mails came within one hour of each other: without any replies from me. An e-mail every hour is not romantic when you have no relationship with the person. It was downright creepy. My gut instinct said to stop all communication immediately. Mike was desperate, and it was no longer a safe environment.

Did I mislead Mike in the beginning by swiftly answering his e-mail messages? Some might say yes; I disagree. Whether I was right or wrong, Mike's reaction was disturbing to say the least, and I had no choice but to terminate the communication. It was a no-brainer. I sent an e-mail that was direct and non-confrontational, as it was not my intent to hurt him. My intent was to end communication. I kept my eye on the prize and did not mince words.

*E-mail message to Mike:*

*"I have decided to terminate our communication as I have decided not to move forward with you. Good luck with your search. **Please do not respond to this message.**"*

# A Trip around the Block

Of course, I received another e-mail message from Mike, and this time it had an aggressive undertone. It was for a Trip around the Block for Mike. I blocked him with no regrets, and I moved on. Use your head, read the undertones, and, most of all, practice safety first.

I had another incident where a guy copied my online introduction and used it in his own profile verbatim, then contacted me. *Oh my!* I wanted so badly to take it as a compliment. I thought maybe he was trying to play a creative game, except that it came off as creepy and didn't feel right. So I blocked him.

In the case that a member demonstrates unfavorable behavior, *The Online Dating Journal* provides an area to document information regarding the blocked member.

> *Tip: Don't be the victim of someone blocking you. Be careful not to become obsessed with a member. If someone is not interested in communicating with you, leave that person alone. Remember, there are literally forty million more registered members where that <u>one</u> came from!*

Please block responsibly.
*Sample log entry for a blocked member:*

| Blocked Member Details |
| --- |
| Block Date: *June 20, 20XX* Method: *I blocked [Member Name] through the [Name of Online Dating Service] Web site* |
| Reason / Details: |
| *Mike constantly sends e-mail messages asking to visit me. Mike is very aggressive and seems to be angry with me because I told him that we need to get to know each other better. On June 20, 20XX, Mike sent eight e-mails within eight hours asking me to visit his home. Very needy, very creepy, very blocked!* |

# The
# Online
# Journey

# The Online Journey I

## Contact Data

Screen Name: _XOXOXOXOXOX_          Legal Name: _Morgan Miller_

Online Dating Service: _[Name of Service]_     Date contact initiated: _August 20, 2005_

☑ I initiated contact     ☐ He/She initiated contact

The reason I made contact or responded to contact:
_I made contact because Morgan is within 25 miles of my location. I do not like long-distance relationships._
_VERY attractive picture!_

## Exchange of Personal Data

Date I sent personal data: _October 29, 20XX_   Date I received personal data: _October 30, 20XX_
Address: _1234 Any Street_            City: _Any City_    State: _XX_     Zip: _11111_
Age: _35_          Height: _5'10_     Other: _____
Contact Numbers:  Home: _555-555-5555_   Mobile: _444-444-4444_   Other: _____
E-mail address: _Morgan@todj.us_

## Photo Overview

Photo ☑ Yes / ☐ No

_I sent Morgan two pictures. The one taken on the cruise and the one in the black suit._
_Morgan sent three pictures. Morgan looked different in each pix, and one was very fuzzy._

## Let the Journey Begin—Number of Correspondence

| ̶I̶I̶I̶ II | Sent to contact | ̶I̶I̶I̶ II | Received from contact |
|---|---|---|---|
| III | E-mail messages | ̶I̶I̶I̶I̶ I | E-mail messages |
| II | Emoticons (winks, smiles, etc.) | III | Emoticons (winks, smiles, etc.) |
| ̶I̶I̶I̶I̶ III | Phone calls | ̶I̶I̶I̶I̶ II | Phone calls |
| I | Virtual dates initiated | II | Virtual dates initiated |
| I | Live dates initiated | I | Live dates initiated |
| | U.S. mail | II | U.S. mail |
| II | Other | I | Other |

## Miscellaneous

_Divorced_
_Children_
_Loves animals_

# The Online Journey II

Member Rating: 1 2 3 4 5 6 7 8 9 10 / ☺ ☺ ☹

Initial thought of profile:

*Very witty, possible match*

Initial thought of correspondence:

*Well-written, interesting*

What I like most:

*Morgan's sense of humor and infectious laughter*

What I like least:

_____

## Comments

Document key information that you want to remember.
*(i.e., great conversationalist, cried on first date, great voice, member looking for long-term relationship, etc.)*

*Our first conversation was great.*
*Loves dogs…almost too much.*
*Has used online dating services for 4 years, a professional dater.*
*Married once for 7 years…Maybe got the itch.*
*Gives great compliments.*
*Grunts a lot! What's that all about? It's kind of annoying.*
*Extrovert in private, introvert in public.*

## Blocked Member Details

Date: _____     Blocking Method: _____

Reasons/Details:

_____
_____
_____

# The Online Journey I

## Contact Data

Screen Name: _____     Legal Name: _____

Online Dating Service: _____     Date contact initiated: _____

☐ I initiated contact     ☐ He/She initiated contact

The reason I made contact or responded to contact:

_____

## Exchange of Personal Data

Date I sent personal data: _____     Date I received personal data: _____

Address: _____     City: _____ State: _____ Zip: _____

Age: _____     Height: _____     Other: _____

Contact Numbers:     Home: _____     Mobile: _____     Other: _____

E-mail address:

## Photo Overview

Photo ☐ Yes / ☐ No

_____

_____

## Let the Journey Begin—Number of Correspondence

| ̶H̶I̶I | Sent to contact | ̶H̶I̶I | Received from contact |
|---|---|---|---|
| | E-mail messages | | E-mail messages |
| | Emoticons (winks, smiles, etc.) | | Emoticons (winks, smiles, etc.) |
| | Phone calls | | Phone calls |
| | Virtual dates initiated | | Virtual dates initiated |
| | Live dates initiated | | Live dates initiated |
| | U.S. mail | | U.S. mail |
| | Other | | Other |

## Miscellaneous

_____

_____

_____

# The Online Journey II

Member Rating: 1 2 3 4 5 6 7 8 9 10 / ☺ ☺ ☹

Initial thought of profile:
_____

Initial thought of correspondence:
_____

What I like most:
_____

What I like least:
_____

## Comments
Document key information that you want to remember.
*(i.e., great conversationalist, cried on first date, great voice, member looking for long-term relationship, etc.)*

_____
_____
_____
_____
_____
_____
_____
_____
_____
_____

## Blocked Member Details

Date: _____    Blocking Method: _____

Reasons/Details:
_____
_____
_____

# The Online Journey I

## Contact Data

Screen Name: _____     Legal Name: _____

Online Dating Service: _____     Date contact initiated: _____

☐ I initiated contact     ☐ He/She initiated contact

The reason I made contact or responded to contact:

_____

## Exchange of Personal Data

Date I sent personal data: _____     Date I received personal data: _____

Address: _____     City: _____     State: _____     Zip: _____

Age: _____     Height: _____     Other: _____

Contact Numbers:     Home: _____     Mobile: _____     Other: _____

E-mail address:

## Photo Overview

Photo ☐ Yes / ☐ No

_____

_____

## Let the Journey Begin—Number of Correspondence

| ⦀ᵗ II | Sent to contact | ⦀ᵗ II | Received from contact |
|---|---|---|---|
| | E-mail messages | | E-mail messages |
| | Emoticons (winks, smiles, etc.) | | Emoticons (winks, smiles, etc.) |
| | Phone calls | | Phone calls |
| | Virtual dates initiated | | Virtual dates initiated |
| | Live dates initiated | | Live dates initiated |
| | U.S. mail | | U.S. mail |
| | Other | | Other |

## Miscellaneous

_____

_____

_____

# The Online Journey II

Member Rating: 1 2 3 4 5 6 7 8 9 10 / ☺ ☺ ☹

Initial thought of profile:
_____

Initial thought of correspondence:
_____

What I like most:
_____

What I like least:
_____

## Comments
Document key information that you want to remember.
*(i.e., great conversationalist, cried on first date, great voice, member looking for long-term relationship, etc.)*

_____
_____
_____
_____
_____
_____
_____
_____
_____

## Blocked Member Details

Date: _____    Blocking Method: _____

Reasons/Details:
_____
_____
_____

# The Online Journey I

| Contact Data |
|---|

Screen Name: _____  Legal Name: _____

Online Dating Service: _____  Date contact initiated: _____

☐ I initiated contact     ☐ He/She initiated contact

The reason I made contact or responded to contact:

_____

| Exchange of Personal Data |
|---|

Date I sent personal data: _____  Date I received personal data: _____

Address: _____  City: _____  State: _____  Zip: _____

Age: _____  Height: _____  Other: _____

Contact Numbers:  Home: _____  Mobile: _____  Other: _____

E-mail address:

| Photo Overview |
|---|

Photo ☐ Yes / ☐ No

_____
_____

| Let the Journey Begin—Number of Correspondence ||||
|---|---|---|---|
| ~~IIII~~ II | Sent to contact | ~~IIII~~ II | Received from contact |
| | E-mail messages | | E-mail messages |
| | Emoticons (winks, smiles, etc.) | | Emoticons (winks, smiles, etc.) |
| | Phone calls | | Phone calls |
| | Virtual dates initiated | | Virtual dates initiated |
| | Live dates initiated | | Live dates initiated |
| | U.S. mail | | U.S. mail |
| | Other | | Other |

| Miscellaneous |
|---|

_____
_____
_____

# The Online Journey II

Initial thought of profile:

_____

Initial thought of correspondence:

_____

What I like most:

_____

What I like least:

_____

## Comments

Document key information that you want to remember.
*(i.e., great conversationalist, cried on first date, great voice, member looking for long-term relationship, etc.)*

_____
_____
_____
_____
_____
_____
_____
_____
_____
_____

## Blocked Member Details

Date: _____   Blocking Method: _____

Reasons/Details:

_____
_____
_____

# The Online Journey I

## Contact Data

Screen Name: _____     Legal Name: _____

Online Dating Service: _____     Date contact initiated: _____

☐ I initiated contact     ☐ He/She initiated contact

The reason I made contact or responded to contact:

_____

## Exchange of Personal Data

Date I sent personal data: _____     Date I received personal data: _____

Address: _____     City: _____ State: _____ Zip: _____

Age: _____     Height: _____     Other: _____

Contact Numbers:     Home: _____     Mobile: _____     Other: _____

E-mail address:

## Photo Overview

Photo ☐ Yes / ☐ No

_____

_____

## Let the Journey Begin—Number of Correspondence

| ~~IIII~~ II | Sent to contact | ~~IIII~~ II | Received from contact |
|---|---|---|---|
| | E-mail messages | | E-mail messages |
| | Emoticons (winks, smiles, etc.) | | Emoticons (winks, smiles, etc.) |
| | Phone calls | | Phone calls |
| | Virtual dates initiated | | Virtual dates initiated |
| | Live dates initiated | | Live dates initiated |
| | U.S. mail | | U.S. mail |
| | Other | | Other |

## Miscellaneous

_____

_____

_____

# The Online Journey II

Initial thought of profile:
_____

Initial thought of correspondence:
_____

What I like most:
_____

What I like least:
_____

## Comments
Document key information that you want to remember.
*(i.e., great conversationalist, cried on first date, great voice, member looking for long-term relationship, etc.)*

_____
_____
_____
_____
_____
_____
_____
_____
_____

## Blocked Member Details

Date: _____    Blocking Method: _____

Reasons/Details:
_____
_____
_____

*Be alive. Live in the moment.*

# The Online Journey I

## Contact Data

Screen Name: _____     Legal Name: _____

Online Dating Service: _____     Date contact initiated: _____

☐ I initiated contact      ☐ He/She initiated contact

The reason I made contact or responded to contact:

_____

## Exchange of Personal Data

Date I sent personal data: _____     Date I received personal data: _____

Address: _____     City: _____     State: _____     Zip: _____

Age: _____     Height: _____     Other: _____

Contact Numbers:     Home: _____     Mobile: _____     Other: _____

E-mail address:

## Photo Overview

Photo ☐ Yes / ☐ No

_____

_____

## Let the Journey Begin—Number of Correspondence

| ‖‖ ‖ | Sent to contact | ‖‖ ‖ | Received from contact |
|---|---|---|---|
|  | E-mail messages |  | E-mail messages |
|  | Emoticons (winks, smiles, etc.) |  | Emoticons (winks, smiles, etc.) |
|  | Phone calls |  | Phone calls |
|  | Virtual dates initiated |  | Virtual dates initiated |
|  | Live dates initiated |  | Live dates initiated |
|  | U.S. mail |  | U.S. mail |
|  | Other |  | Other |

## Miscellaneous

_____

_____

_____

# The Online Journey II

Initial thought of profile:
_____

Initial thought of correspondence:
_____

What I like most:
_____

What I like least:
_____

## Comments

Document key information that you want to remember.
*(i.e., great conversationalist, cried on first date, great voice, member looking for long-term relationship, etc.)*

_____
_____
_____
_____
_____
_____
_____
_____
_____
_____

## Blocked Member Details

Date: _____     Blocking Method: _____

Reasons/Details:
_____
_____
_____

# The Online Journey I

## Contact Data

Screen Name: _____     Legal Name: _____

Online Dating Service: _____     Date contact initiated: _____

☐ I initiated contact     ☐ He/She initiated contact

The reason I made contact or responded to contact:

_____

## Exchange of Personal Data

Date I sent personal data: _____     Date I received personal data: _____

Address: _____     City: _____ State: _____ Zip: _____

Age: _____ Height: _____     Other: _____

Contact Numbers:   Home: _____     Mobile: _____ Other: _____

E-mail address:

## Photo Overview

Photo ☐ Yes / ☐ No

_____
_____

## Let the Journey Begin—Number of Correspondence

| JHT II | Sent to contact | JHT II | Received from contact |
|---|---|---|---|
| | E-mail messages | | E-mail messages |
| | Emoticons (winks, smiles, etc.) | | Emoticons (winks, smiles, etc.) |
| | Phone calls | | Phone calls |
| | Virtual dates initiated | | Virtual dates initiated |
| | Live dates initiated | | Live dates initiated |
| | U.S. mail | | U.S. mail |
| | Other | | Other |

## Miscellaneous

_____
_____
_____

# The Online Journey II

Member Rating: 1 2 3 4 5 6 7 8 9 10 / ☺ ☺ ☹

Initial thought of profile:
_____

Initial thought of correspondence:
_____

What I like most:
_____

What I like least:
_____

## Comments

Document key information that you want to remember.
*(i.e., great conversationalist, cried on first date, great voice, member looking for long-term relationship, etc.)*

_____
_____
_____
_____
_____
_____
_____
_____
_____
_____
_____

## Blocked Member Details

Date: _____    Blocking Method: _____

Reasons/Details:
_____
_____
_____

# The Online Journey I

## Contact Data

Screen Name: _____     Legal Name: _____

Online Dating Service: _____     Date contact initiated: _____

☐ I initiated contact     ☐ He/She initiated contact

The reason I made contact or responded to contact:

_____

## Exchange of Personal Data

Date I sent personal data: _____     Date I received personal data: _____

Address: _____     City: _____  State: _____  Zip: _____

Age: _____     Height: _____     Other: _____

Contact Numbers:     Home: _____     Mobile: _____  Other: _____

E-mail address:

## Photo Overview

Photo ☐ Yes / ☐ No

_____

_____

## Let the Journey Begin—Number of Correspondence

| ||||||  || | Sent to contact | ||||||  || | Received from contact |
|---|---|---|---|
| | E-mail messages | | E-mail messages |
| | Emoticons (winks, smiles, etc.) | | Emoticons (winks, smiles, etc.) |
| | Phone calls | | Phone calls |
| | Virtual dates initiated | | Virtual dates initiated |
| | Live dates initiated | | Live dates initiated |
| | U.S. mail | | U.S. mail |
| | Other | | Other |

## Miscellaneous

_____

_____

_____

# The Online Journey II

Initial thought of profile:
_____

Initial thought of correspondence:
_____

What I like most:
_____

What I like least:
_____

## Comments

Document key information that you want to remember.
*(i.e., great conversationalist, cried on first date, great voice, member looking for long-term relationship, etc.)*

_____
_____
_____
_____
_____
_____
_____
_____
_____
_____

## Blocked Member Details

Date: _____    Blocking Method: _____

Reasons/Details:
_____
_____
_____

# The Online Journey I

## Contact Data

Screen Name: _____     Legal Name: _____

Online Dating Service: _____     Date contact initiated: _____

☐ I initiated contact     ☐ He/She initiated contact

The reason I made contact or responded to contact:

_____

## Exchange of Personal Data

Date I sent personal data: _____    Date I received personal data: _____

Address: _____    City: _____ State: _____ Zip: _____

Age: _____    Height: _____    Other: _____

Contact Numbers:   Home: _____    Mobile: _____   Other: _____

E-mail address:

## Photo Overview

Photo ☐ Yes / ☐ No

_____

_____

## Let the Journey Begin—Number of Correspondence

| ɪɪɪɪ ɪɪ | Sent to contact | ɪɪɪɪ ɪɪ | Received from contact |
|---|---|---|---|
| | E-mail messages | | E-mail messages |
| | Emoticons (winks, smiles, etc.) | | Emoticons (winks, smiles, etc.) |
| | Phone calls | | Phone calls |
| | Virtual dates initiated | | Virtual dates initiated |
| | Live dates initiated | | Live dates initiated |
| | U.S. mail | | U.S. mail |
| | Other | | Other |

## Miscellaneous

_____

_____

_____

# The Online Journey II

Member Rating: 1 2 3 4 5 6 7 8 9 10 / ☺ ☺ ☹

Initial thought of profile:
_____

Initial thought of correspondence:
_____

What I like most:
_____

What I like least:
_____

## Comments

Document key information that you want to remember.
*(i.e., great conversationalist, cried on first date, great voice, member looking for long-term relationship, etc.)*

_____
_____
_____
_____
_____
_____
_____
_____

## Blocked Member Details

Date: _____    Blocking Method: _____

Reasons/Details:
_____
_____
_____

# The Online Journey I

## Contact Data

Screen Name: _____  Legal Name: _____

Online Dating Service: _____  Date contact initiated: _____

☐ I initiated contact    ☐ He/She initiated contact

The reason I made contact or responded to contact:

_____

## Exchange of Personal Data

Date I sent personal data: _____  Date I received personal data: _____

Address: _____  City: _____  State: _____  Zip: _____

Age: _____  Height: _____  Other: _____

Contact Numbers:    Home: _____  Mobile: _____  Other: _____

E-mail address:

## Photo Overview

Photo ☐ Yes / ☐ No

_____

_____

## Let the Journey Begin—Number of Correspondence

| |̷H̷T̷ II| Sent to contact | |̷H̷T̷ II| Received from contact |
|---|---|---|---|
| | E-mail messages | | E-mail messages |
| | Emoticons (winks, smiles, etc.) | | Emoticons (winks, smiles, etc.) |
| | Phone calls | | Phone calls |
| | Virtual dates initiated | | Virtual dates initiated |
| | Live dates initiated | | Live dates initiated |
| | U.S. mail | | U.S. mail |
| | Other | | Other |

## Miscellaneous

_____

_____

_____

# The Online Journey II

Initial thought of profile:

_____

Initial thought of correspondence:

_____

What I like most:

_____

What I like least:

_____

## Comments

Document key information that you want to remember.
*(i.e., great conversationalist, cried on first date, great voice, member looking for long-term relationship, etc.)*

_____
_____
_____
_____
_____
_____
_____
_____
_____

## Blocked Member Details

Date: _____    Blocking Method: _____

Reasons/Details:

_____
_____
_____

*Take time to enjoy life's simple pleasures.*

# The Online Journey I

## Contact Data

Screen Name: _____  Legal Name: _____

Online Dating Service: _____  Date contact initiated: _____

☐ I initiated contact     ☐ He/She initiated contact

The reason I made contact or responded to contact:

_____

## Exchange of Personal Data

Date I sent personal data: _____  Date I received personal data: _____

Address: _____  City: _____ State: _____ Zip: _____

Age: _____  Height: _____  Other: _____

Contact Numbers:  Home: _____  Mobile: _____  Other: _____

E-mail address:

## Photo Overview

Photo ☐ Yes / ☐ No

_____

_____

## Let the Journey Begin—Number of Correspondence

| IIII II | Sent to contact | IIII II | Received from contact |
|---|---|---|---|
| | E-mail messages | | E-mail messages |
| | Emoticons (winks, smiles, etc.) | | Emoticons (winks, smiles, etc.) |
| | Phone calls | | Phone calls |
| | Virtual dates initiated | | Virtual dates initiated |
| | Live dates initiated | | Live dates initiated |
| | U.S. mail | | U.S. mail |
| | Other | | Other |

## Miscellaneous

_____

_____

_____

# The Online Journey II

Initial thought of profile:
_____

Initial thought of correspondence:
_____

What I like most:
_____

What I like least:
_____

## Comments

Document key information that you want to remember.
*(i.e., great conversationalist, cried on first date, great voice, member looking for long-term relationship, etc.)*

_____
_____
_____
_____
_____
_____
_____
_____
_____

## Blocked Member Details

Date: _____     Blocking Method: _____

Reasons/Details:
_____
_____
_____

# The Online Journey I

## Contact Data

Screen Name: _____  Legal Name: _____

Online Dating Service: _____  Date contact initiated: _____

☐ I initiated contact    ☐ He/She initiated contact

The reason I made contact or responded to contact:

_____

## Exchange of Personal Data

Date I sent personal data: _____  Date I received personal data: _____

Address: _____  City: _____  State: _____  Zip: _____

Age: _____  Height: _____  Other: _____

Contact Numbers:  Home: _____  Mobile: _____  Other: _____

E-mail address:

### Photo Overview

Photo ☐ Yes / ☐ No

_____

_____

## Let the Journey Begin—Number of Correspondence

| ̶I̶I̶I̶ II | Sent to contact | ̶I̶I̶I̶ II | Received from contact |
|---|---|---|---|
| | E-mail messages | | E-mail messages |
| | Emoticons (winks, smiles, etc.) | | Emoticons (winks, smiles, etc.) |
| | Phone calls | | Phone calls |
| | Virtual dates initiated | | Virtual dates initiated |
| | Live dates initiated | | Live dates initiated |
| | U.S. mail | | U.S. mail |
| | Other | | Other |

## Miscellaneous

_____

_____

_____

# The Online Journey II

Member Rating: 1 2 3 4 5 6 7 8 9 10 / ☺ ☺ ☹

Initial thought of profile:
_____

Initial thought of correspondence:
_____

What I like most:
_____

What I like least:
_____

## Comments

Document key information that you want to remember.
*(i.e., great conversationalist, cried on first date, great voice, member looking for long-term relationship, etc.)*

_____
_____
_____
_____
_____
_____
_____
_____
_____

## Blocked Member Details

Date: _____    Blocking Method: _____

Reasons/Details:
_____
_____
_____

Friends
are sometimes better than
lovers.

List the lasting friendships that you have formed as a result of online dating.

_____

_____

_____

_____

_____

_____

_____

_____

# The Online Journey I

## Contact Data

Screen Name: _____     Legal Name: _____

Online Dating Service: _____     Date contact initiated: _____

☐ I initiated contact     ☐ He/She initiated contact

The reason I made contact or responded to contact:

_____

## Exchange of Personal Data

Date I sent personal data: _____     Date I received personal data: _____

Address: _____     City: _____     State: _____     Zip: _____

Age: _____     Height: _____     Other: _____

Contact Numbers:     Home: _____     Mobile: _____     Other: _____

E-mail address:

## Photo Overview

Photo ☐ Yes / ☐ No

_____

_____

## Let the Journey Begin—Number of Correspondence

| ꓤꓤꓤ II | Sent to contact | ꓤꓤꓤ II | Received from contact |
|---|---|---|---|
| | E-mail messages | | E-mail messages |
| | Emoticons (winks, smiles, etc.) | | Emoticons (winks, smiles, etc.) |
| | Phone calls | | Phone calls |
| | Virtual dates initiated | | Virtual dates initiated |
| | Live dates initiated | | Live dates initiated |
| | U.S. mail | | U.S. mail |
| | Other | | Other |

## Miscellaneous

_____

_____

_____

# The Online Journey II

Initial thought of profile:

_____

Initial thought of correspondence:

_____

What I like most:

_____

What I like least:

_____

## Comments

Document key information that you want to remember.
*(i.e., great conversationalist, cried on first date, great voice, member looking for long-term relationship, etc.)*

_____
_____
_____
_____
_____
_____
_____
_____
_____

## Blocked Member Details

Date: _____     Blocking Method: _____

Reasons/Details:

_____
_____
_____

# The Online Journey I

## Contact Data

Screen Name: _____    Legal Name: _____

Online Dating Service: _____    Date contact initiated: _____

☐ I initiated contact       ☐ He/She initiated contact

The reason I made contact or responded to contact:

_____

## Exchange of Personal Data

Date I sent personal data: _____    Date I received personal data: _____

Address: _____    City: _____ State: _____ Zip: _____

Age: _____    Height: _____    Other: _____

Contact Numbers:    Home: _____    Mobile: _____    Other: _____

E-mail address:

## Photo Overview

Photo ☐ Yes / ☐ No

_____

_____

## Let the Journey Begin—Number of Correspondence

| ⊬ ‖ | Sent to contact | ⊬ ‖ | Received from contact |
|---|---|---|---|
| | E-mail messages | | E-mail messages |
| | Emoticons (winks, smiles, etc.) | | Emoticons (winks, smiles, etc.) |
| | Phone calls | | Phone calls |
| | Virtual dates initiated | | Virtual dates initiated |
| | Live dates initiated | | Live dates initiated |
| | U.S. mail | | U.S. mail |
| | Other | | Other |

## Miscellaneous

_____

_____

_____

# The Online Journey II

Initial thought of profile:
_____

Initial thought of correspondence:
_____

What I like most:
_____

What I like least:
_____

## Comments

Document key information that you want to remember.
*(i.e., great conversationalist, cried on first date, great voice, member looking for long-term relationship, etc.)*

_____
_____
_____
_____
_____
_____
_____
_____
_____
_____

## Blocked Member Details

Date: _____     Blocking Method: _____

Reasons/Details:
_____
_____
_____

*It's your life. You do not have to make excuses.*

# The Online Journey I

## Contact Data

Screen Name: _____    Legal Name: _____

Online Dating Service: _____    Date contact initiated: _____

☐ I initiated contact    ☐ He/She initiated contact

The reason I made contact or responded to contact:

_____

## Exchange of Personal Data

Date I sent personal data: _____    Date I received personal data: _____

Address: _____    City: _____ State: _____ Zip: _____

Age: _____    Height: _____    Other: _____

Contact Numbers:   Home: _____    Mobile: _____ Other: _____

E-mail address:

### Photo Overview

Photo ☐ Yes / ☐ No

_____
_____

## Let the Journey Begin—Number of Correspondence

| ̶H̶T̶ II | Sent to contact | ̶H̶T̶ II | Received from contact |
|---|---|---|---|
| | E-mail messages | | E-mail messages |
| | Emoticons (winks, smiles, etc.) | | Emoticons (winks, smiles, etc.) |
| | Phone calls | | Phone calls |
| | Virtual dates initiated | | Virtual dates initiated |
| | Live dates initiated | | Live dates initiated |
| | U.S. mail | | U.S. mail |
| | Other | | Other |

## Miscellaneous

_____
_____
_____

# The Online Journey II

Initial thought of profile:
_____

Initial thought of correspondence:
_____

What I like most:
_____

What I like least:
_____

## Comments

Document key information that you want to remember.
*(i.e., great conversationalist, cried on first date, great voice, member looking for long-term relationship, etc.)*

_____
_____
_____
_____
_____
_____
_____
_____
_____
_____

## Blocked Member Details

Date: _____    Blocking Method: _____

Reasons/Details:
_____
_____
_____

# The Online Journey I

## Contact Data

Screen Name: _____     Legal Name: _____

Online Dating Service: _____     Date contact initiated: _____

☐ I initiated contact     ☐ He/She initiated contact

The reason I made contact or responded to contact:

_____

## Exchange of Personal Data

Date I sent personal data: _____     Date I received personal data: _____

Address: _____     City: _____   State: _____   Zip: _____

Age: _____     Height: _____     Other: _____

Contact Numbers:     Home: _____     Mobile: _____     Other: _____

E-mail address:

## Photo Overview

Photo ☐ Yes / ☐ No

_____
_____

## Let the Journey Begin—Number of Correspondence

| ||||| || | Sent to contact | ||||| || | Received from contact |
|---|---|---|---|
| | E-mail messages | | E-mail messages |
| | Emoticons (winks, smiles, etc.) | | Emoticons (winks, smiles, etc.) |
| | Phone calls | | Phone calls |
| | Virtual dates initiated | | Virtual dates initiated |
| | Live dates initiated | | Live dates initiated |
| | U.S. mail | | U.S. mail |
| | Other | | Other |

## Miscellaneous

_____
_____
_____

# The Online Journey II

Initial thought of profile:
_____

Initial thought of correspondence:
_____

What I like most:
_____

What I like least:
_____

## Comments

Document key information that you want to remember.
*(i.e., great conversationalist, cried on first date, great voice, member looking for long-term relationship, etc.)*

_____
_____
_____
_____
_____
_____
_____
_____
_____
_____

## Blocked Member Details

Date: _____    Blocking Method: _____

Reasons/Details:
_____
_____
_____

# The Online Journey I

## Contact Data

Screen Name: _____     Legal Name: _____

Online Dating Service: _____     Date contact initiated: _____

☐ I initiated contact     ☐ He/She initiated contact

The reason I made contact or responded to contact:

_____

## Exchange of Personal Data

Date I sent personal data: _____     Date I received personal data: _____

Address: _____     City: _____     State: _____     Zip: _____

Age: _____     Height: _____     Other: _____

Contact Numbers:     Home: _____     Mobile: _____     Other: _____

E-mail address:

## Photo Overview

Photo ☐ Yes / ☐ No

_____

_____

## Let the Journey Begin—Number of Correspondence

| ~~IIII~~ II | Sent to contact | ~~IIII~~ II | Received from contact |
|---|---|---|---|
| | E-mail messages | | E-mail messages |
| | Emoticons (winks, smiles, etc.) | | Emoticons (winks, smiles, etc.) |
| | Phone calls | | Phone calls |
| | Virtual dates initiated | | Virtual dates initiated |
| | Live dates initiated | | Live dates initiated |
| | U.S. mail | | U.S. mail |
| | Other | | Other |

## Miscellaneous

_____

_____

_____

# The Online Journey II

Member Rating: 1 2 3 4 5 6 7 8 9 10 / ☺ ☺ ☹

Initial thought of profile:
_____

Initial thought of correspondence:
_____

What I like most:
_____

What I like least:
_____

## Comments

Document key information that you want to remember.
*(i.e., great conversationalist, cried on first date, great voice, member looking for long-term relationship, etc.)*

_____
_____
_____
_____
_____
_____
_____
_____

## Blocked Member Details

Date: _____    Blocking Method: _____

Reasons/Details:
_____
_____
_____

# The Online Journey I

## Contact Data

Screen Name: _____  Legal Name: _____

Online Dating Service: _____  Date contact initiated: _____

☐ I initiated contact　　☐ He/She initiated contact

The reason I made contact or responded to contact:

_____

## Exchange of Personal Data

Date I sent personal data: _____  Date I received personal data: _____

Address: _____  City: _____  State: _____  Zip: _____

Age: _____  Height: _____  Other: _____

Contact Numbers:　Home: _____  Mobile: _____  Other: _____

E-mail address:

## Photo Overview

Photo ☐ Yes / ☐ No

_____

_____

## Let the Journey Begin—Number of Correspondence

| ⦀⧼ II | Sent to contact | ⦀⧼ II | Received from contact |
|---|---|---|---|
|  | E-mail messages |  | E-mail messages |
|  | Emoticons (winks, smiles, etc.) |  | Emoticons (winks, smiles, etc.) |
|  | Phone calls |  | Phone calls |
|  | Virtual dates initiated |  | Virtual dates initiated |
|  | Live dates initiated |  | Live dates initiated |
|  | U.S. mail |  | U.S. mail |
|  | Other |  | Other |

## Miscellaneous

_____

_____

_____

# The Online Journey II

Member Rating: 1 2 3 4 5 6 7 8 9 10 / ☺ ☺ ☹

Initial thought of profile:
_____

Initial thought of correspondence:
_____

What I like most:
_____

What I like least:
_____

## Comments

Document key information that you want to remember.
*(i.e., great conversationalist, cried on first date, great voice, member looking for long-term relationship, etc.)*

_____
_____
_____
_____
_____
_____
_____
_____
_____

## Blocked Member Details

Date: _____     Blocking Method: _____

Reasons/Details:
_____
_____
_____

# The Online Journey I

## Contact Data

Screen Name: _____    Legal Name: _____

Online Dating Service: _____    Date contact initiated: _____

☐ I initiated contact    ☐ He/She initiated contact

The reason I made contact or responded to contact:

_____

## Exchange of Personal Data

Date I sent personal data: _____    Date I received personal data: _____

Address: _____    City: _____ State: _____ Zip: _____

Age: _____    Height: _____    Other: _____

Contact Numbers:   Home: _____    Mobile: _____   Other: _____

E-mail address:

### Photo Overview

Photo ☐ Yes / ☐ No

_____
_____

## Let the Journey Begin—Number of Correspondence

| ~~IIII~~ II | Sent to contact | ~~IIII~~ II | Received from contact |
|---|---|---|---|
| | E-mail messages | | E-mail messages |
| | Emoticons (winks, smiles, etc.) | | Emoticons (winks, smiles, etc.) |
| | Phone calls | | Phone calls |
| | Virtual dates initiated | | Virtual dates initiated |
| | Live dates initiated | | Live dates initiated |
| | U.S. mail | | U.S. mail |
| | Other | | Other |

## Miscellaneous

_____
_____
_____

# The Online Journey II

Initial thought of profile:
_____

Initial thought of correspondence:
_____

What I like most:
_____

What I like least:
_____

## Comments

Document key information that you want to remember.
*(i.e., great conversationalist, cried on first date, great voice, member looking for long-term relationship, etc.)*

_____
_____
_____
_____
_____
_____
_____
_____
_____

## Blocked Member Details

Date: _____     Blocking Method: _____

Reasons/Details:
_____
_____
_____

*Respect the differences in others.*

# The Online Journey I

| | Contact Data | |
|---|---|---|

Screen Name: _____     Legal Name: _____

Online Dating Service: _____     Date contact initiated: _____

☐ I initiated contact      ☐ He/She initiated contact

The reason I made contact or responded to contact:

_____

| Exchange of Personal Data |
|---|

Date I sent personal data: _____     Date I received personal data: _____

Address: _____     City: _____ State: _____ Zip: _____

Age: _____     Height: _____     Other: _____

Contact Numbers:     Home: _____     Mobile: _____ Other: _____

E-mail address:

| Photo Overview |
|---|

Photo ☐ Yes / ☐ No

_____

_____

| | Let the Journey Begin—Number of Correspondence | | |
|---|---|---|---|
| ɪɪɪɪ̷ ıı | Sent to contact | ɪɪɪɪ̷ ıı | Received from contact |
| | E-mail messages | | E-mail messages |
| | Emoticons (winks, smiles, etc.) | | Emoticons (winks, smiles, etc.) |
| | Phone calls | | Phone calls |
| | Virtual dates initiated | | Virtual dates initiated |
| | Live dates initiated | | Live dates initiated |
| | U.S. mail | | U.S. mail |
| | Other | | Other |

| Miscellaneous |
|---|

_____

_____

_____

## The Online Journey II

Member Rating: 1 2 3 4 5 6 7 8 9 10 / ☺ ☺ ☹

Initial thought of profile:

_____

Initial thought of correspondence:

_____

What I like most:

_____

What I like least:

_____

### Comments

Document key information that you want to remember.
*(i.e., great conversationalist, cried on first date, great voice, member looking for long-term relationship, etc.)*

_____
_____
_____
_____
_____
_____
_____
_____
_____

### Blocked Member Details

Date: _____    Blocking Method: _____

Reasons/Details:

_____
_____
_____

# The Online Journey I

## Contact Data

Screen Name: _____  Legal Name: _____

Online Dating Service: _____  Date contact initiated: _____

☐ I initiated contact    ☐ He/She initiated contact

The reason I made contact or responded to contact:

_____

## Exchange of Personal Data

Date I sent personal data: _____  Date I received personal data: _____

Address: _____  City: _____  State: _____  Zip: _____

Age: _____   Height: _____  Other: _____

Contact Numbers:   Home: _____  Mobile: _____  Other: _____

E-mail address:

## Photo Overview

Photo ☐ Yes / ☐ No

_____

_____

## Let the Journey Begin—Number of Correspondence

| 卌 II | Sent to contact | 卌 II | Received from contact |
|---|---|---|---|
|  | E-mail messages |  | E-mail messages |
|  | Emoticons (winks, smiles, etc.) |  | Emoticons (winks, smiles, etc.) |
|  | Phone calls |  | Phone calls |
|  | Virtual dates initiated |  | Virtual dates initiated |
|  | Live dates initiated |  | Live dates initiated |
|  | U.S. mail |  | U.S. mail |
|  | Other |  | Other |

## Miscellaneous

_____

_____

_____

# The Online Journey II

Initial thought of profile:

_____

Initial thought of correspondence:

_____

What I like most:

_____

What I like least:

_____

## Comments

Document key information that you want to remember.
*(i.e., great conversationalist, cried on first date, great voice, member looking for long-term relationship, etc.)*

_____
_____
_____
_____
_____
_____
_____
_____
_____

## Blocked Member Details

Date: _____    Blocking Method: _____

Reasons/Details:

_____
_____
_____

# The Online Journey I

## Contact Data

Screen Name: _____     Legal Name: _____

Online Dating Service: _____     Date contact initiated: _____

☐ I initiated contact     ☐ He/She initiated contact

The reason I made contact or responded to contact:

_____

## Exchange of Personal Data

Date I sent personal data: _____     Date I received personal data: _____

Address: _____     City: _____ State: _____ Zip: _____

Age: _____     Height: _____     Other: _____

Contact Numbers:     Home: _____     Mobile: _____ Other: _____

E-mail address:

### Photo Overview

Photo ☐ Yes / ☐ No

_____

_____

## Let the Journey Begin—Number of Correspondence

| ⳾H̶T̶ II | Sent to contact | ⳾H̶T̶ II | Received from contact |
|---|---|---|---|
|  | E-mail messages |  | E-mail messages |
|  | Emoticons (winks, smiles, etc.) |  | Emoticons (winks, smiles, etc.) |
|  | Phone calls |  | Phone calls |
|  | Virtual dates initiated |  | Virtual dates initiated |
|  | Live dates initiated |  | Live dates initiated |
|  | U.S. mail |  | U.S. mail |
|  | Other |  | Other |

## Miscellaneous

_____

_____

_____

# The Online Journey II

Member Rating: 1 2 3 4 5 6 7 8 9 10 / ☺ ☺ ☹

Initial thought of profile:

_____

Initial thought of correspondence:

_____

What I like most:

_____

What I like least:

_____

## Comments

Document key information that you want to remember.
*(i.e., great conversationalist, cried on first date, great voice, member looking for long-term relationship, etc.)*

_____
_____
_____
_____
_____
_____
_____
_____
_____

## Blocked Member Details

Date: _____     Blocking Method: _____

Reasons/Details:

_____
_____
_____

# The Online Journey I

## Contact Data

Screen Name: _____     Legal Name: _____

Online Dating Service: _____     Date contact initiated: _____

☐ I initiated contact     ☐ He/She initiated contact

The reason I made contact or responded to contact:

_____

## Exchange of Personal Data

Date I sent personal data: _____     Date I received personal data: _____

Address: _____     City: _____     State: _____     Zip: _____

Age: _____     Height: _____     Other: _____

Contact Numbers:     Home: _____     Mobile: _____     Other: _____

E-mail address:

## Photo Overview

Photo ☐ Yes / ☐ No

_____

_____

## Let the Journey Begin—Number of Correspondence

| ~~IIII~~ II | Sent to contact | ~~IIII~~ II | Received from contact |
|---|---|---|---|
| | E-mail messages | | E-mail messages |
| | Emoticons (winks, smiles, etc.) | | Emoticons (winks, smiles, etc.) |
| | Phone calls | | Phone calls |
| | Virtual dates initiated | | Virtual dates initiated |
| | Live dates initiated | | Live dates initiated |
| | U.S. mail | | U.S. mail |
| | Other | | Other |

## Miscellaneous

_____

_____

_____

# The Online Journey II

Member Rating: 1 2 3 4 5 6 7 8 9 10 / ☺ ☺ ☹

Initial thought of profile:
_____

Initial thought of correspondence:
_____

What I like most:
_____

What I like least:
_____

## Comments

Document key information that you want to remember.
*(i.e., great conversationalist, cried on first date, great voice, member looking for long-term relationship, etc.)*

_____
_____
_____
_____
_____
_____
_____
_____
_____

## Blocked Member Details

Date: _____    Blocking Method: _____

Reasons/Details:
_____
_____
_____

# The Online Journey I

## Contact Data

Screen Name: _____  Legal Name: _____

Online Dating Service: _____  Date contact initiated: _____

☐ I initiated contact    ☐ He/She initiated contact

The reason I made contact or responded to contact:

_____

## Exchange of Personal Data

Date I sent personal data: _____  Date I received personal data: _____

Address: _____  City: _____  State: _____  Zip: _____

Age: _____  Height: _____  Other: _____

Contact Numbers:  Home: _____  Mobile: _____  Other: _____

E-mail address:

## Photo Overview

Photo ☐ Yes / ☐ No

_____

_____

## Let the Journey Begin—Number of Correspondence

| ЖΙΙ | Sent to contact | ЖΙΙ | Received from contact |
|---|---|---|---|
| | E-mail messages | | E-mail messages |
| | Emoticons (winks, smiles, etc.) | | Emoticons (winks, smiles, etc.) |
| | Phone calls | | Phone calls |
| | Virtual dates initiated | | Virtual dates initiated |
| | Live dates initiated | | Live dates initiated |
| | U.S. mail | | U.S. mail |
| | Other | | Other |

## Miscellaneous

_____

_____

_____

# The Online Journey II

Initial thought of profile:
_____

Initial thought of correspondence:
_____

What I like most:
_____

What I like least:
_____

## Comments

Document key information that you want to remember.
*(i.e., great conversationalist, cried on first date, great voice, member looking for long-term relationship, etc.)*

_____
_____
_____
_____
_____
_____
_____
_____
_____
_____

## Blocked Member Details

Date: _____     Blocking Method: _____

Reasons/Details:
_____
_____
_____

*Nothing inspires like hope.*

# The Online Journey I

## Contact Data

Screen Name: _____     Legal Name: _____

Online Dating Service: _____     Date contact initiated: _____

☐ I initiated contact     ☐ He/She initiated contact

The reason I made contact or responded to contact:

_____

## Exchange of Personal Data

Date I sent personal data: _____     Date I received personal data: _____

Address: _____     City: _____  State: _____  Zip: _____

Age: _____     Height: _____     Other: _____

Contact Numbers:     Home: _____     Mobile: _____  Other: _____

E-mail address:

## Photo Overview

Photo ☐ Yes / ☐ No

_____

_____

## Let the Journey Begin—Number of Correspondence

| ⲦⲦ̷ II | Sent to contact | ⲦⲦ̷ II | Received from contact |
|---|---|---|---|
| | E-mail messages | | E-mail messages |
| | Emoticons (winks, smiles, etc.) | | Emoticons (winks, smiles, etc.) |
| | Phone calls | | Phone calls |
| | Virtual dates initiated | | Virtual dates initiated |
| | Live dates initiated | | Live dates initiated |
| | U.S. mail | | U.S. mail |
| | Other | | Other |

## Miscellaneous

_____

_____

_____

# The Online Journey II

Member Rating: 1 2 3 4 5 6 7 8 9 10 / ☺ ☺ ☹

Initial thought of profile:
_____

Initial thought of correspondence:
_____

What I like most:
_____

What I like least:
_____

## Comments

Document key information that you want to remember.
*(i.e., great conversationalist, cried on first date, great voice, member looking for long-term relationship, etc.)*

_____
_____
_____
_____
_____
_____
_____
_____
_____

## Blocked Member Details

Date: _____  Blocking Method: _____

Reasons/Details:
_____
_____
_____

# The Online Journey I

## Contact Data

Screen Name: _____     Legal Name: _____

Online Dating Service: _____     Date contact initiated: _____

☐ I initiated contact     ☐ He/She initiated contact

The reason I made contact or responded to contact:

_____

## Exchange of Personal Data

Date I sent personal data: _____     Date I received personal data: _____

Address: _____     City: _____  State: _____  Zip: _____

Age: _____     Height: _____     Other: _____

Contact Numbers:     Home: _____     Mobile: _____  Other: _____

E-mail address:

## Photo Overview

Photo ☐ Yes / ☐ No

_____

_____

## Let the Journey Begin—Number of Correspondence

| ||||| || | Sent to contact | ||||| || | Received from contact |
|---|---|---|---|
| | E-mail messages | | E-mail messages |
| | Emoticons (winks, smiles, etc.) | | Emoticons (winks, smiles, etc.) |
| | Phone calls | | Phone calls |
| | Virtual dates initiated | | Virtual dates initiated |
| | Live dates initiated | | Live dates initiated |
| | U.S. mail | | U.S. mail |
| | Other | | Other |

## Miscellaneous

_____

_____

_____

# The Online Journey II

## Member Rating: 1 2 3 4 5 6 7 8 9 10 / ☺ ☻ ☹

Initial thought of profile:

_____

Initial thought of correspondence:

_____

What I like most:

_____

What I like least:

_____

## Comments

Document key information that you want to remember.
*(i.e., great conversationalist, cried on first date, great voice, member looking for long-term relationship, etc.)*

_____
_____
_____
_____
_____
_____
_____
_____
_____

## Blocked Member Details

Date: _____     Blocking Method: _____

Reasons/Details:

_____
_____
_____

# The Online Journey I

## Contact Data

Screen Name: _____     Legal Name: _____

Online Dating Service: _____     Date contact initiated: _____

☐ I initiated contact     ☐ He/She initiated contact

The reason I made contact or responded to contact:

_____

## Exchange of Personal Data

Date I sent personal data: _____     Date I received personal data: _____

Address: _____     City: _____  State: _____  Zip: _____

Age: _____     Height: _____     Other: _____

Contact Numbers:     Home: _____     Mobile: _____  Other: _____

E-mail address:

## Photo Overview

Photo ☐ Yes / ☐ No

_____

_____

## Let the Journey Begin—Number of Correspondence

| ~~JHT~~ II | Sent to contact | ~~JHT~~ II | Received from contact |
|---|---|---|---|
| | E-mail messages | | E-mail messages |
| | Emoticons (winks, smiles, etc.) | | Emoticons (winks, smiles, etc.) |
| | Phone calls | | Phone calls |
| | Virtual dates initiated | | Virtual dates initiated |
| | Live dates initiated | | Live dates initiated |
| | U.S. mail | | U.S. mail |
| | Other | | Other |

## Miscellaneous

_____

_____

_____

# The Online Journey II

Member Rating: 1 2 3 4 5 6 7 8 9 10 / ☺ ☻ ☹

Initial thought of profile:

_____

Initial thought of correspondence:

_____

What I like most:

_____

What I like least:

_____

## Comments

Document key information that you want to remember.
*(i.e., great conversationalist, cried on first date, great voice, member looking for long-term relationship, etc.)*

_____
_____
_____
_____
_____
_____
_____
_____
_____

## Blocked Member Details

Date: _____    Blocking Method: _____

Reasons/Details:

_____
_____
_____

# The Online Journey I

## Contact Data

Screen Name: _____     Legal Name: _____

Online Dating Service: _____     Date contact initiated: _____

☐ I initiated contact     ☐ He/She initiated contact

The reason I made contact or responded to contact:

_____

## Exchange of Personal Data

Date I sent personal data: _____     Date I received personal data: _____

Address: _____     City: _____     State: _____     Zip: _____

Age: _____     Height: _____     Other: _____

Contact Numbers:     Home: _____     Mobile: _____     Other: _____

E-mail address:

### Photo Overview

Photo ☐ Yes / ☐ No

_____

_____

## Let the Journey Begin—Number of Correspondence

| ⊬⊬ II | Sent to contact | ⊬⊬ II | Received from contact |
|---|---|---|---|
| | E-mail messages | | E-mail messages |
| | Emoticons (winks, smiles, etc.) | | Emoticons (winks, smiles, etc.) |
| | Phone calls | | Phone calls |
| | Virtual dates initiated | | Virtual dates initiated |
| | Live dates initiated | | Live dates initiated |
| | U.S. mail | | U.S. mail |
| | Other | | Other |

## Miscellaneous

_____

_____

_____

# The Online Journey II

Initial thought of profile:
_____

Initial thought of correspondence:
_____

What I like most:
_____

What I like least:
_____

## Comments
Document key information that you want to remember.
*(i.e., great conversationalist, cried on first date, great voice, member looking for long-term relationship, etc.)*

_____
_____
_____
_____
_____
_____
_____
_____
_____
_____

## Blocked Member Details

Date: _____     Blocking Method: _____

Reasons/Details:
_____
_____
_____

# The Online Journey I

## Contact Data

Screen Name: _____     Legal Name: _____

Online Dating Service: _____     Date contact initiated: _____

☐ I initiated contact     ☐ He/She initiated contact

The reason I made contact or responded to contact:

_____

## Exchange of Personal Data

Date I sent personal data: _____     Date I received personal data: _____

Address: _____     City: _____     State: _____     Zip: _____

Age: _____     Height: _____     Other: _____

Contact Numbers:     Home: _____     Mobile: _____     Other: _____

E-mail address:

## Photo Overview

Photo ☐ Yes / ☐ No

_____

_____

## Let the Journey Begin—Number of Correspondence

| ~~IIII~~ II | Sent to contact | ~~IIII~~ II | Received from contact |
|---|---|---|---|
| | E-mail messages | | E-mail messages |
| | Emoticons (winks, smiles, etc.) | | Emoticons (winks, smiles, etc.) |
| | Phone calls | | Phone calls |
| | Virtual dates initiated | | Virtual dates initiated |
| | Live dates initiated | | Live dates initiated |
| | U.S. mail | | U.S. mail |
| | Other | | Other |

## Miscellaneous

_____

_____

_____

# The Online Journey II

Member Rating: 1 2 3 4 5 6 7 8 9 10 / ☺ ☺ ☹

Initial thought of profile:
_____

Initial thought of correspondence:
_____

What I like most:
_____

What I like least:
_____

## Comments

Document key information that you want to remember.
*(i.e., great conversationalist, cried on first date, great voice, member looking for long-term relationship, etc.)*

_____
_____
_____
_____
_____
_____
_____
_____
_____
_____
_____

## Blocked Member Details

Date: _____    Blocking Method: _____

Reasons/Details:
_____
_____
_____

*Never lose your integrity; it is impossible to regain.*

# The Online Journey I

## Contact Data

Screen Name: _____ Legal Name: _____

Online Dating Service: _____ Date contact initiated: _____

☐ I initiated contact ☐ He/She initiated contact

The reason I made contact or responded to contact:

_____

## Exchange of Personal Data

Date I sent personal data: _____ Date I received personal data: _____

Address: _____ City: _____ State: _____ Zip: _____

Age: _____ Height: _____ Other: _____

Contact Numbers: Home: _____ Mobile: _____ Other: _____

E-mail address:

### Photo Overview

Photo ☐ Yes / ☐ No

_____

_____

## Let the Journey Begin—Number of Correspondence

| ЦНТ ‖ | Sent to contact | ЦНТ ‖ | Received from contact |
|---|---|---|---|
| | E-mail messages | | E-mail messages |
| | Emoticons (winks, smiles, etc.) | | Emoticons (winks, smiles, etc.) |
| | Phone calls | | Phone calls |
| | Virtual dates initiated | | Virtual dates initiated |
| | Live dates initiated | | Live dates initiated |
| | U.S. mail | | U.S. mail |
| | Other | | Other |

## Miscellaneous

_____

_____

_____

# The Online Journey II

Initial thought of profile:
_____

Initial thought of correspondence:
_____

What I like most:
_____

What I like least:
_____

## Comments

Document key information that you want to remember.
*(i.e., great conversationalist, cried on first date, great voice, member looking for long-term relationship, etc.)*

_____
_____
_____
_____
_____
_____
_____
_____
_____

## Blocked Member Details

Date: _____     Blocking Method: _____

Reasons/Details:
_____
_____
_____

# The Online Journey I

## Contact Data

Screen Name: _____    Legal Name: _____

Online Dating Service: _____    Date contact initiated: _____

☐ I initiated contact      ☐ He/She initiated contact

The reason I made contact or responded to contact:

_____

## Exchange of Personal Data

Date I sent personal data: _____    Date I received personal data: _____

Address: _____    City: _____  State: _____  Zip: _____

Age: _____    Height: _____    Other: _____

Contact Numbers:    Home: _____    Mobile: _____    Other: _____

E-mail address:

## Photo Overview

Photo ☐ Yes / ☐ No

_____

_____

## Let the Journey Begin—Number of Correspondence

| ~~IIII~~ II | Sent to contact | ~~IIII~~ II | Received from contact |
|---|---|---|---|
|  | E-mail messages |  | E-mail messages |
|  | Emoticons (winks, smiles, etc.) |  | Emoticons (winks, smiles, etc.) |
|  | Phone calls |  | Phone calls |
|  | Virtual dates initiated |  | Virtual dates initiated |
|  | Live dates initiated |  | Live dates initiated |
|  | U.S. mail |  | U.S. mail |
|  | Other |  | Other |

## Miscellaneous

_____

_____

_____

# The Online Journey II

Member Rating: 1 2 3 4 5 6 7 8 9 10 / ☺ ☺ ☹

Initial thought of profile:

_____

Initial thought of correspondence:

_____

What I like most:

_____

What I like least:

_____

## Comments

Document key information that you want to remember.
*(i.e., great conversationalist, cried on first date, great voice, member looking for long-term relationship, etc.)*

_____
_____
_____
_____
_____
_____
_____
_____
_____

## Blocked Member Details

Date: _____    Blocking Method: _____

Reasons/Details:

_____
_____
_____

# The Online Journey I

## Contact Data

Screen Name: _____   Legal Name: _____

Online Dating Service: _____   Date contact initiated: _____

☐ I initiated contact    ☐ He/She initiated contact

The reason I made contact or responded to contact:

_____

## Exchange of Personal Data

Date I sent personal data: _____   Date I received personal data: _____

Address: _____   City: _____   State: _____   Zip: _____

Age: _____   Height: _____   Other: _____

Contact Numbers:   Home: _____   Mobile: _____   Other: _____

E-mail address:

### Photo Overview

Photo ☐ Yes / ☐ No

_____

_____

## Let the Journey Begin—Number of Correspondence

| ̶I̶I̶I̶ II | Sent to contact | ̶I̶I̶I̶ II | Received from contact |
|---|---|---|---|
| | E-mail messages | | E-mail messages |
| | Emoticons (winks, smiles, etc.) | | Emoticons (winks, smiles, etc.) |
| | Phone calls | | Phone calls |
| | Virtual dates initiated | | Virtual dates initiated |
| | Live dates initiated | | Live dates initiated |
| | U.S. mail | | U.S. mail |
| | Other | | Other |

## Miscellaneous

_____

_____

_____

# The Online Journey II

Initial thought of profile:

_____

Initial thought of correspondence:

_____

What I like most:

_____

What I like least:

_____

## Comments

Document key information that you want to remember.
*(i.e., great conversationalist, cried on first date, great voice, member looking for long-term relationship, etc.)*

_____
_____
_____
_____
_____
_____
_____
_____
_____
_____

## Blocked Member Details

Date: _____    Blocking Method: _____

Reasons/Details:

_____
_____
_____

Make *every* date
a memorable experience.

List five things that you can do to enhance your online dating experiences.

_____

_____

_____

_____

_____

# The Online Journey I

## Contact Data

Screen Name: _____    Legal Name: _____

Online Dating Service: _____    Date contact initiated: _____

☐ I initiated contact        ☐ He/She initiated contact

The reason I made contact or responded to contact:

_____

## Exchange of Personal Data

Date I sent personal data: _____    Date I received personal data: _____

Address: _____    City: _____ State: _____ Zip: _____

Age: _____    Height: _____    Other: _____

Contact Numbers:    Home: _____    Mobile: _____    Other: _____

E-mail address:

## Photo Overview

Photo ☐ Yes / ☐ No

_____

_____

## Let the Journey Begin—Number of Correspondence

| ⠶⃥ II | Sent to contact | ⠶⃥ II | Received from contact |
|---|---|---|---|
| | E-mail messages | | E-mail messages |
| | Emoticons (winks, smiles, etc.) | | Emoticons (winks, smiles, etc.) |
| | Phone calls | | Phone calls |
| | Virtual dates initiated | | Virtual dates initiated |
| | Live dates initiated | | Live dates initiated |
| | U.S. mail | | U.S. mail |
| | Other | | Other |

## Miscellaneous

_____

_____

_____

# The Online Journey II

Member Rating: 1 2 3 4 5 6 7 8 9 10 / ☺ ☺ ☹

Initial thought of profile:
_____

Initial thought of correspondence:
_____

What I like most:
_____

What I like least:
_____

## Comments

Document key information that you want to remember.
*(i.e., great conversationalist, cried on first date, great voice, member looking for long-term relationship, etc.)*

_____
_____
_____
_____
_____
_____
_____
_____
_____
_____

## Blocked Member Details

Date: _____      Blocking Method: _____

Reasons/Details:
_____
_____
_____

*Take time to make lasting connections.*

# The Online Journey I

## Contact Data

Screen Name: _____     Legal Name: _____

Online Dating Service: _____     Date contact initiated: _____

☐ I initiated contact     ☐ He/She initiated contact

The reason I made contact or responded to contact:

_____

## Exchange of Personal Data

Date I sent personal data: _____     Date I received personal data: _____

Address: _____     City: _____     State: _____     Zip: _____

Age: _____     Height: _____     Other: _____

Contact Numbers:     Home: _____     Mobile: _____     Other: _____

E-mail address:

## Photo Overview

Photo ☐ Yes / ☐ No

_____

_____

## Let the Journey Begin—Number of Correspondence

| ~~IIII~~ II | Sent to contact | ~~IIII~~ II | Received from contact |
|---|---|---|---|
| | E-mail messages | | E-mail messages |
| | Emoticons (winks, smiles, etc.) | | Emoticons (winks, smiles, etc.) |
| | Phone calls | | Phone calls |
| | Virtual dates initiated | | Virtual dates initiated |
| | Live dates initiated | | Live dates initiated |
| | U.S. mail | | U.S. mail |
| | Other | | Other |

## Miscellaneous

_____

_____

_____

# The Online Journey II

Initial thought of profile:
_____

Initial thought of correspondence:
_____

What I like most:
_____

What I like least:
_____

## Comments

Document key information that you want to remember.
*(i.e., great conversationalist, cried on first date, great voice, member looking for long-term relationship, etc.)*

_____
_____
_____
_____
_____
_____
_____
_____
_____

## Blocked Member Details

Date: _____    Blocking Method: _____

Reasons/Details:
_____
_____
_____

# The Online Journey I

## Contact Data

Screen Name: _____    Legal Name: _____

Online Dating Service: _____    Date contact initiated: _____

☐ I initiated contact    ☐ He/She initiated contact

The reason I made contact or responded to contact:

_____

## Exchange of Personal Data

Date I sent personal data: _____    Date I received personal data: _____

Address: _____    City: _____    State: _____    Zip: _____

Age: _____    Height: _____    Other: _____

Contact Numbers:    Home: _____    Mobile: _____    Other: _____

E-mail address:

## Photo Overview

Photo ☐ Yes / ☐ No

_____

_____

## Let the Journey Begin—Number of Correspondence

| ~~IIII~~ II | Sent to contact | ~~IIII~~ II | Received from contact |
|---|---|---|---|
| | E-mail messages | | E-mail messages |
| | Emoticons (winks, smiles, etc.) | | Emoticons (winks, smiles, etc.) |
| | Phone calls | | Phone calls |
| | Virtual dates initiated | | Virtual dates initiated |
| | Live dates initiated | | Live dates initiated |
| | U.S. mail | | U.S. mail |
| | Other | | Other |

## Miscellaneous

_____

_____

_____

# The Online Journey II

Member Rating: 1 2 3 4 5 6 7 8 9 10 / ☺ ☺ ☹

Initial thought of profile:

_____

Initial thought of correspondence:

_____

What I like most:

_____

What I like least:

_____

## Comments

Document key information that you want to remember.
*(i.e., great conversationalist, cried on first date, great voice, member looking for long-term relationship, etc.)*

_____
_____
_____
_____
_____
_____
_____
_____
_____

## Blocked Member Details

Date: _____    Blocking Method: _____

Reasons/Details:

_____
_____
_____

# The Online Journey I

## Contact Data

Screen Name: _____  Legal Name: _____

Online Dating Service: _____  Date contact initiated: _____

☐ I initiated contact    ☐ He/She initiated contact

The reason I made contact or responded to contact:

_____

## Exchange of Personal Data

Date I sent personal data: _____  Date I received personal data: _____

Address: _____  City: _____  State: _____  Zip: _____

Age: _____    Height: _____    Other: _____

Contact Numbers:    Home: _____    Mobile: _____    Other: _____

E-mail address:

### Photo Overview

Photo ☐ Yes / ☐ No

_____

_____

## Let the Journey Begin—Number of Correspondence

| ~~IIII~~ II | Sent to contact | ~~IIII~~ II | Received from contact |
|---|---|---|---|
| | E-mail messages | | E-mail messages |
| | Emoticons (winks, smiles, etc.) | | Emoticons (winks, smiles, etc.) |
| | Phone calls | | Phone calls |
| | Virtual dates initiated | | Virtual dates initiated |
| | Live dates initiated | | Live dates initiated |
| | U.S. mail | | U.S. mail |
| | Other | | Other |

## Miscellaneous

_____

_____

_____

# The Online Journey II

Initial thought of profile:

_____

Initial thought of correspondence:

_____

What I like most:

_____

What I like least:

_____

## Comments
### Document key information that you want to remember.
*(i.e., great conversationalist, cried on first date, great voice, member looking for long-term relationship, etc.)*

_____
_____
_____
_____
_____
_____
_____
_____

## Blocked Member Details

Date: _____   Blocking Method: _____

Reasons/Details:

_____
_____
_____

# The Online Journey I

## Contact Data

Screen Name: _____ Legal Name: _____

Online Dating Service: _____ Date contact initiated: _____

☐ I initiated contact    ☐ He/She initiated contact

The reason I made contact or responded to contact:

_____

## Exchange of Personal Data

Date I sent personal data: _____ Date I received personal data: _____

Address: _____ City: _____ State: _____ Zip: _____

Age: _____ Height: _____ Other: _____

Contact Numbers: Home: _____ Mobile: _____ Other: _____

E-mail address:

## Photo Overview

Photo ☐ Yes / ☐ No

_____

_____

## Let the Journey Begin—Number of Correspondence

| ЖН II | Sent to contact | ЖН II | Received from contact |
|---|---|---|---|
| | E-mail messages | | E-mail messages |
| | Emoticons (winks, smiles, etc.) | | Emoticons (winks, smiles, etc.) |
| | Phone calls | | Phone calls |
| | Virtual dates initiated | | Virtual dates initiated |
| | Live dates initiated | | Live dates initiated |
| | U.S. mail | | U.S. mail |
| | Other | | Other |

## Miscellaneous

_____

_____

_____

# The Online Journey II

Initial thought of profile:
_____

Initial thought of correspondence:
_____

What I like most:
_____

What I like least:
_____

## Comments

Document key information that you want to remember.
*(i.e., great conversationalist, cried on first date, great voice, member looking for long-term relationship, etc.)*

_____
_____
_____
_____
_____
_____
_____
_____
_____
_____

## Blocked Member Details

Date: _____     Blocking Method: _____

Reasons/Details:
_____
_____
_____

# The Online Journey I

## Contact Data

Screen Name: _____     Legal Name: _____

Online Dating Service: _____     Date contact initiated: _____

☐ I initiated contact     ☐ He/She initiated contact

The reason I made contact or responded to contact:

_____

## Exchange of Personal Data

Date I sent personal data: _____     Date I received personal data: _____

Address: _____     City: _____   State: _____   Zip: _____

Age: _____     Height: _____     Other: _____

Contact Numbers:     Home: _____     Mobile: _____     Other: _____

E-mail address:

## Photo Overview

Photo ☐ Yes / ☐ No

_____

_____

## Let the Journey Begin—Number of Correspondence

| ~~‖‖~~ ‖ | Sent to contact | ~~‖‖~~ ‖ | Received from contact |
|---|---|---|---|
| | E-mail messages | | E-mail messages |
| | Emoticons (winks, smiles, etc.) | | Emoticons (winks, smiles, etc.) |
| | Phone calls | | Phone calls |
| | Virtual dates initiated | | Virtual dates initiated |
| | Live dates initiated | | Live dates initiated |
| | U.S. mail | | U.S. mail |
| | Other | | Other |

## Miscellaneous

_____

_____

_____

# The Online Journey II

Member Rating: 1 2 3 4 5 6 7 8 9 10 / ☺ ☺ ☹

Initial thought of profile:
_____

Initial thought of correspondence:
_____

What I like most:
_____

What I like least:
_____

## Comments

Document key information that you want to remember.
*(i.e., great conversationalist, cried on first date, great voice, member looking for long-term relationship, etc.)*

_____
_____
_____
_____
_____
_____
_____
_____
_____

## Blocked Member Details

Date: _____    Blocking Method: _____

Reasons/Details:
_____
_____
_____

*Not everyone will be a match, but you can learn something from everyone.*

# The Online Journey I

## Contact Data

Screen Name: _____   Legal Name: _____

Online Dating Service: _____   Date contact initiated: _____

☐ I initiated contact    ☐ He/She initiated contact

The reason I made contact or responded to contact:

_____

## Exchange of Personal Data

Date I sent personal data: _____   Date I received personal data: _____

Address: _____   City: _____   State: _____   Zip: _____

Age: _____   Height: _____   Other: _____

Contact Numbers:   Home: _____   Mobile: _____   Other: _____

E-mail address:

## Photo Overview

Photo ☐ Yes / ☐ No

_____

_____

## Let the Journey Begin—Number of Correspondence

| ~~|||| || | Sent to contact | ~~|||| || | Received from contact |
|---|---|---|---|
| | E-mail messages | | E-mail messages |
| | Emoticons (winks, smiles, etc.) | | Emoticons (winks, smiles, etc.) |
| | Phone calls | | Phone calls |
| | Virtual dates initiated | | Virtual dates initiated |
| | Live dates initiated | | Live dates initiated |
| | U.S. mail | | U.S. mail |
| | Other | | Other |

## Miscellaneous

_____

_____

_____

# The Online Journey II

Member Rating: 1 2 3 4 5 6 7 8 9 10 / ☺ ☺ ☹

Initial thought of profile:
_____

Initial thought of correspondence:
_____

What I like most:
_____

What I like least:
_____

## Comments

Document key information that you want to remember.
*(i.e., great conversationalist, cried on first date, great voice, member looking for long-term relationship, etc.)*

_____
_____
_____
_____
_____
_____
_____
_____
_____

## Blocked Member Details

Date: _____    Blocking Method: _____

Reasons/Details:
_____
_____
_____

# The Online Journey I

## Contact Data

Screen Name: _____ Legal Name: _____

Online Dating Service: _____ Date contact initiated: _____

☐ I initiated contact     ☐ He/She initiated contact

The reason I made contact or responded to contact:

_____

## Exchange of Personal Data

Date I sent personal data: _____ Date I received personal data: _____

Address: _____ City: _____ State: _____ Zip: _____

Age: _____ Height: _____ Other: _____

Contact Numbers:   Home: _____ Mobile: _____ Other: _____

E-mail address:

## Photo Overview

Photo ☐ Yes / ☐ No

_____

_____

## Let the Journey Begin—Number of Correspondence

| ~~IIII~~ II | Sent to contact | ~~IIII~~ II | Received from contact |
|---|---|---|---|
| | E-mail messages | | E-mail messages |
| | Emoticons (winks, smiles, etc.) | | Emoticons (winks, smiles, etc.) |
| | Phone calls | | Phone calls |
| | Virtual dates initiated | | Virtual dates initiated |
| | Live dates initiated | | Live dates initiated |
| | U.S. mail | | U.S. mail |
| | Other | | Other |

## Miscellaneous

_____

_____

_____

# The Online Journey II

Member Rating: 1 2 3 4 5 6 7 8 9 10 / ☺ ☺ ☹

Initial thought of profile:

_____

Initial thought of correspondence:

_____

What I like most:

_____

What I like least:

_____

## Comments

Document key information that you want to remember.
*(i.e., great conversationalist, cried on first date, great voice, member looking for long-term relationship, etc.)*

_____
_____
_____
_____
_____
_____
_____
_____
_____
_____

## Blocked Member Details

Date: _____     Blocking Method: _____

Reasons/Details:

_____
_____
_____

# The Online Journey I

## Contact Data

Screen Name: ____________________ Legal Name: ____________________

Online Dating Service: ____________ Date contact initiated: ____________

☐ I initiated contact ☐ He/She initiated contact

The reason I made contact or responded to contact:

________________________________________________

## Exchange of Personal Data

Date I sent personal data: ____________ Date I received personal data: ____________

Address: ____________________ City: ________ State: ______ Zip: ______

Age: ________ Height: ________ Other: ____________________

Contact Numbers: Home: ________ Mobile: ____________ Other: ________

E-mail address:

## Photo Overview

Photo ☐ Yes / ☐ No

________________________________________________

________________________________________________

## Let the Journey Begin—Number of Correspondence

| 𝍸 II | Sent to contact | 𝍸 II | Received from contact |
|---|---|---|---|
| | E-mail messages | | E-mail messages |
| | Emoticons (winks, smiles, etc.) | | Emoticons (winks, smiles, etc.) |
| | Phone calls | | Phone calls |
| | Virtual dates initiated | | Virtual dates initiated |
| | Live dates initiated | | Live dates initiated |
| | U.S. mail | | U.S. mail |
| | Other | | Other |

## Miscellaneous

________________________________________________

________________________________________________

________________________________________________

# The Online Journey II

Initial thought of profile:

_____

Initial thought of correspondence:

_____

What I like most:

_____

What I like least:

_____

## Comments
Document key information that you want to remember.
*(i.e., great conversationalist, cried on first date, great voice, member looking for long-term relationship, etc.)*

_____
_____
_____
_____
_____
_____
_____
_____
_____
_____

## Blocked Member Details

Date: _____    Blocking Method: _____

Reasons/Details:

_____
_____
_____

# The Online Journey I

## Contact Data

Screen Name: _____  Legal Name: _____

Online Dating Service: _____  Date contact initiated: _____

☐ I initiated contact    ☐ He/She initiated contact

The reason I made contact or responded to contact:

_____

## Exchange of Personal Data

Date I sent personal data: _____  Date I received personal data: _____

Address: _____  City: _____ State: _____ Zip: _____

Age: _____  Height: _____  Other: _____

Contact Numbers:  Home: _____  Mobile: _____ Other: _____

E-mail address:

## Photo Overview

Photo ☐ Yes / ☐ No

_____

_____

## Let the Journey Begin—Number of Correspondence

| ~~IIII~~ II | Sent to contact | ~~IIII~~ II | Received from contact |
|---|---|---|---|
| | E-mail messages | | E-mail messages |
| | Emoticons (winks, smiles, etc.) | | Emoticons (winks, smiles, etc.) |
| | Phone calls | | Phone calls |
| | Virtual dates initiated | | Virtual dates initiated |
| | Live dates initiated | | Live dates initiated |
| | U.S. mail | | U.S. mail |
| | Other | | Other |

## Miscellaneous

_____

_____

_____

# The Online Journey II

Initial thought of profile:
_____

Initial thought of correspondence:
_____

What I like most:
_____

What I like least:
_____

## Comments

Document key information that you want to remember.
*(i.e., great conversationalist, cried on first date, great voice, member looking for long-term relationship, etc.)*

_____
_____
_____
_____
_____
_____
_____
_____
_____

## Blocked Member Details

Date: _____    Blocking Method: _____

Reasons/Details:
_____
_____
_____

# The Online Journey I

## Contact Data

Screen Name: _____    Legal Name: _____

Online Dating Service: _____    Date contact initiated: _____

☐ I initiated contact    ☐ He/She initiated contact

The reason I made contact or responded to contact:

_____

## Exchange of Personal Data

Date I sent personal data: _____    Date I received personal data: _____

Address: _____    City: _____ State: _____ Zip: _____

Age: _____    Height: _____    Other: _____

Contact Numbers:    Home: _____    Mobile: _____    Other: _____

E-mail address:

## Photo Overview

Photo ☐ Yes / ☐ No

_____

_____

## Let the Journey Begin—Number of Correspondence

| ~~IIII~~ II | Sent to contact | ~~IIII~~ II | Received from contact |
|---|---|---|---|
| | E-mail messages | | E-mail messages |
| | Emoticons (winks, smiles, etc.) | | Emoticons (winks, smiles, etc.) |
| | Phone calls | | Phone calls |
| | Virtual dates initiated | | Virtual dates initiated |
| | Live dates initiated | | Live dates initiated |
| | U.S. mail | | U.S. mail |
| | Other | | Other |

## Miscellaneous

_____

_____

_____

# The Online Journey II

Member Rating: 1 2 3 4 5 6 7 8 9 10 / ☺ ☺ ☹

Initial thought of profile:

_____

Initial thought of correspondence:

_____

What I like most:

_____

What I like least:

_____

## Comments

Document key information that you want to remember.
*(i.e., great conversationalist, cried on first date, great voice, member looking for long-term relationship, etc.)*

_____
_____
_____
_____
_____
_____
_____
_____
_____
_____

## Blocked Member Details

Date: _____  Blocking Method: _____

Reasons/Details:

_____
_____
_____

*No one's perfect. You can only strive to be your very best.*

# The Online Journey I

## Contact Data

Screen Name: _____ Legal Name: _____

Online Dating Service: _____ Date contact initiated: _____

☐ I initiated contact    ☐ He/She initiated contact

The reason I made contact or responded to contact:

_____

## Exchange of Personal Data

Date I sent personal data: _____ Date I received personal data: _____

Address: _____ City: _____ State: _____ Zip: _____

Age: _____ Height: _____ Other: _____

Contact Numbers:   Home: _____ Mobile: _____ Other: _____

E-mail address:

## Photo Overview

Photo ☐ Yes / ☐ No

_____

_____

## Let the Journey Begin—Number of Correspondence

| ~~IIII~~ II | Sent to contact | ~~IIII~~ II | Received from contact |
|---|---|---|---|
| | E-mail messages | | E-mail messages |
| | Emoticons (winks, smiles, etc.) | | Emoticons (winks, smiles, etc.) |
| | Phone calls | | Phone calls |
| | Virtual dates initiated | | Virtual dates initiated |
| | Live dates initiated | | Live dates initiated |
| | U.S. mail | | U.S. mail |
| | Other | | Other |

## Miscellaneous

_____

_____

_____

# The Online Journey II

Initial thought of profile:
_____

Initial thought of correspondence:
_____

What I like most:
_____

What I like least:
_____

## Comments

Document key information that you want to remember.
*(i.e., great conversationalist, cried on first date, great voice, member looking for long-term relationship, etc.)*

_____
_____
_____
_____
_____
_____
_____
_____
_____
_____

## Blocked Member Details

Date: _____     Blocking Method: _____

Reasons/Details:
_____
_____
_____

# The Online Journey I

## Contact Data

Screen Name: _____     Legal Name: _____

Online Dating Service: _____     Date contact initiated: _____

☐ I initiated contact     ☐ He/She initiated contact

The reason I made contact or responded to contact:

_____

## Exchange of Personal Data

Date I sent personal data: _____     Date I received personal data: _____

Address: _____     City: _____ State: _____ Zip: _____

Age: _____     Height: _____     Other: _____

Contact Numbers:     Home: _____     Mobile: _____     Other: _____

E-mail address:

## Photo Overview

### Photo ☐ Yes / ☐ No

_____

_____

## Let the Journey Begin—Number of Correspondence

| ̶|̶|̶|̶| II | Sent to contact | ̶|̶|̶|̶| II | Received from contact |
|---|---|---|---|
| | E-mail messages | | E-mail messages |
| | Emoticons (winks, smiles, etc.) | | Emoticons (winks, smiles, etc.) |
| | Phone calls | | Phone calls |
| | Virtual dates initiated | | Virtual dates initiated |
| | Live dates initiated | | Live dates initiated |
| | U.S. mail | | U.S. mail |
| | Other | | Other |

## Miscellaneous

_____

_____

_____

# The Online Journey II

**Member Rating:** 1 2 3 4 5 6 7 8 9 10 / ☺ ☻ ☹

Initial thought of profile:

_____

Initial thought of correspondence:

_____

What I like most:

_____

What I like least:

_____

## Comments
### Document key information that you want to remember.
*(i.e., great conversationalist, cried on first date, great voice, member looking for long-term relationship, etc.)*

_____
_____
_____
_____
_____
_____
_____
_____
_____
_____

## Blocked Member Details

Date: _____ Blocking Method: _____

Reasons/Details:

_____
_____
_____

# The Online Journey I

## Contact Data

Screen Name: _____     Legal Name: _____

Online Dating Service: _____     Date contact initiated: _____

☐ I initiated contact     ☐ He/She initiated contact

The reason I made contact or responded to contact:

_____

## Exchange of Personal Data

Date I sent personal data: _____     Date I received personal data: _____

Address: _____     City: _____ State: _____ Zip: _____

Age: _____     Height: _____     Other: _____

Contact Numbers:     Home: _____     Mobile: _____ Other: _____

E-mail address:

## Photo Overview

Photo ☐ Yes / ☐ No

_____
_____

## Let the Journey Begin—Number of Correspondence

| ̶L̶H̶T̶ II | Sent to contact | ̶L̶H̶T̶ II | Received from contact |
|---|---|---|---|
| | E-mail messages | | E-mail messages |
| | Emoticons (winks, smiles, etc.) | | Emoticons (winks, smiles, etc.) |
| | Phone calls | | Phone calls |
| | Virtual dates initiated | | Virtual dates initiated |
| | Live dates initiated | | Live dates initiated |
| | U.S. mail | | U.S. mail |
| | Other | | Other |

## Miscellaneous

_____
_____
_____

# The Online Journey II

Member Rating: 1 2 3 4 5 6 7 8 9 10 / ☺ ☺ ☹

Initial thought of profile:

_____

Initial thought of correspondence:

_____

What I like most:

_____

What I like least:

_____

## Comments

Document key information that you want to remember.
*(i.e., great conversationalist, cried on first date, great voice, member looking for long-term relationship, etc.)*

_____
_____
_____
_____
_____
_____
_____
_____
_____

## Blocked Member Details

Date: _____    Blocking Method: _____

Reasons/Details:

_____
_____
_____

# The Online Journey I

## Contact Data

Screen Name: _____     Legal Name: _____

Online Dating Service: _____     Date contact initiated: _____

☐ I initiated contact     ☐ He/She initiated contact

The reason I made contact or responded to contact:

_____

## Exchange of Personal Data

Date I sent personal data: _____     Date I received personal data: _____

Address: _____     City: _____  State: _____  Zip: _____

Age: _____     Height: _____     Other: _____

Contact Numbers:     Home: _____     Mobile: _____  Other: _____

E-mail address:

## Photo Overview

Photo ☐ Yes / ☐ No

_____

_____

## Let the Journey Begin—Number of Correspondence

| ~~IIII~~ II | Sent to contact | ~~IIII~~ II | Received from contact |
|---|---|---|---|
| | E-mail messages | | E-mail messages |
| | Emoticons (winks, smiles, etc.) | | Emoticons (winks, smiles, etc.) |
| | Phone calls | | Phone calls |
| | Virtual dates initiated | | Virtual dates initiated |
| | Live dates initiated | | Live dates initiated |
| | U.S. mail | | U.S. mail |
| | Other | | Other |

## Miscellaneous

_____

_____

_____

# The Online Journey II

## Member Rating: 1 2 3 4 5 6 7 8 9 10 / ☺ ☺ ☹

Initial thought of profile:
_____

Initial thought of correspondence:
_____

What I like most:
_____

What I like least:
_____

## Comments

Document key information that you want to remember.
*(i.e., great conversationalist, cried on first date, great voice, member looking for long-term relationship, etc.)*

_____
_____
_____
_____
_____
_____
_____
_____
_____

## Blocked Member Details

Date: _____    Blocking Method: _____

Reasons/Details:
_____
_____
_____

# The Online Journey I

## Contact Data

Screen Name: _____    Legal Name: _____

Online Dating Service: _____    Date contact initiated: _____

☐ I initiated contact      ☐ He/She initiated contact

The reason I made contact or responded to contact:

_____

## Exchange of Personal Data

Date I sent personal data: _____    Date I received personal data: _____

Address: _____    City: _____  State: _____  Zip: _____

Age: _____      Height: _____    Other: _____

Contact Numbers:    Home: _____    Mobile: _____    Other: _____

E-mail address:

## Photo Overview

Photo ☐ Yes / ☐ No

_____

_____

## Let the Journey Begin—Number of Correspondence

| ⊬ʜ ‖ | Sent to contact | ⊬ʜ ‖ | Received from contact |
|---|---|---|---|
| | E-mail messages | | E-mail messages |
| | Emoticons (winks, smiles, etc.) | | Emoticons (winks, smiles, etc.) |
| | Phone calls | | Phone calls |
| | Virtual dates initiated | | Virtual dates initiated |
| | Live dates initiated | | Live dates initiated |
| | U.S. mail | | U.S. mail |
| | Other | | Other |

## Miscellaneous

_____

_____

_____

# The Online Journey II

Initial thought of profile:
_____

Initial thought of correspondence:
_____

What I like most:
_____

What I like least:
_____

## Comments

Document key information that you want to remember.
*(i.e., great conversationalist, cried on first date, great voice, member looking for long-term relationship, etc.)*

_____
_____
_____
_____
_____
_____
_____
_____
_____

## Blocked Member Details

Date: _____     Blocking Method: _____

Reasons/Details:
_____
_____
_____

*Open your mind as you open your heart.*

# The Online Journey I

## Contact Data

Screen Name: _____    Legal Name: _____

Online Dating Service: _____    Date contact initiated: _____

☐ I initiated contact    ☐ He/She initiated contact

The reason I made contact or responded to contact:

_____

## Exchange of Personal Data

Date I sent personal data: _____    Date I received personal data: _____

Address: _____    City: _____  State: _____  Zip: _____

Age: _____    Height: _____    Other: _____

Contact Numbers:    Home: _____    Mobile: _____    Other: _____

E-mail address:

## Photo Overview

Photo ☐ Yes / ☐ No

_____

_____

## Let the Journey Begin—Number of Correspondence

| ⊮ ‖ | Sent to contact | ⊮ ‖ | Received from contact |
|---|---|---|---|
| | E-mail messages | | E-mail messages |
| | Emoticons (winks, smiles, etc.) | | Emoticons (winks, smiles, etc.) |
| | Phone calls | | Phone calls |
| | Virtual dates initiated | | Virtual dates initiated |
| | Live dates initiated | | Live dates initiated |
| | U.S. mail | | U.S. mail |
| | Other | | Other |

## Miscellaneous

_____

_____

_____

# The Online Journey II

Initial thought of profile:

_____

Initial thought of correspondence:

_____

What I like most:

_____

What I like least:

_____

## Comments
Document key information that you want to remember.
*(i.e., great conversationalist, cried on first date, great voice, member looking for long-term relationship, etc.)*

_____
_____
_____
_____
_____
_____
_____
_____
_____
_____

## Blocked Member Details

Date: _____    Blocking Method: _____

Reasons/Details:

_____
_____
_____

# The Online Journey I

## Contact Data

Screen Name: _____     Legal Name: _____

Online Dating Service: _____     Date contact initiated: _____

☐ I initiated contact     ☐ He/She initiated contact

The reason I made contact or responded to contact:

_____

## Exchange of Personal Data

Date I sent personal data: _____     Date I received personal data: _____

Address: _____     City: _____  State: _____  Zip: _____

Age: _____     Height: _____     Other: _____

Contact Numbers:     Home: _____     Mobile: _____     Other: _____

E-mail address:

## Photo Overview

Photo ☐ Yes / ☐ No

_____

_____

## Let the Journey Begin—Number of Correspondence

| ~~IIII~~ II | Sent to contact | ~~IIII~~ II | Received from contact |
|---|---|---|---|
| | E-mail messages | | E-mail messages |
| | Emoticons (winks, smiles, etc.) | | Emoticons (winks, smiles, etc.) |
| | Phone calls | | Phone calls |
| | Virtual dates initiated | | Virtual dates initiated |
| | Live dates initiated | | Live dates initiated |
| | U.S. mail | | U.S. mail |
| | Other | | Other |

## Miscellaneous

_____

_____

_____

# The Online Journey II

Initial thought of profile:
_____

Initial thought of correspondence:
_____

What I like most:
_____

What I like least:
_____

## Comments

Document key information that you want to remember.
*(i.e., great conversationalist, cried on first date, great voice, member looking for long-term relationship, etc.)*

_____
_____
_____
_____
_____
_____
_____
_____
_____
_____

## Blocked Member Details

Date: _____    Blocking Method: _____

Reasons/Details:
_____
_____
_____

# The Online Journey I

## Contact Data

Screen Name: _____    Legal Name: _____

Online Dating Service: _____    Date contact initiated: _____

☐ I initiated contact     ☐ He/She initiated contact

The reason I made contact or responded to contact:

_____

## Exchange of Personal Data

Date I sent personal data: _____    Date I received personal data: _____

Address: _____    City: _____ State: _____ Zip: _____

Age: _____ Height: _____    Other: _____

Contact Numbers:   Home: _____    Mobile: _____ Other: _____

E-mail address:

## Photo Overview

Photo ☐ Yes / ☐ No

_____

_____

## Let the Journey Begin—Number of Correspondence

| ЖT II | Sent to contact | ЖT II | Received from contact |
|---|---|---|---|
| | E-mail messages | | E-mail messages |
| | Emoticons (winks, smiles, etc.) | | Emoticons (winks, smiles, etc.) |
| | Phone calls | | Phone calls |
| | Virtual dates initiated | | Virtual dates initiated |
| | Live dates initiated | | Live dates initiated |
| | U.S. mail | | U.S. mail |
| | Other | | Other |

## Miscellaneous

_____

_____

_____

# The Online Journey II

Initial thought of profile:

_____

Initial thought of correspondence:

_____

What I like most:

_____

What I like least:

_____

## Comments

Document key information that you want to remember.
*(i.e., great conversationalist, cried on first date, great voice, member looking for long-term relationship, etc.)*

_____
_____
_____
_____
_____
_____
_____
_____
_____
_____

## Blocked Member Details

Date: _____     Blocking Method: _____

Reasons/Details:

_____
_____
_____

# The Online Journey I

## Contact Data

Screen Name: _____     Legal Name: _____

Online Dating Service: _____     Date contact initiated: _____

☐ I initiated contact     ☐ He/She initiated contact

The reason I made contact or responded to contact:

_____
_____

## Exchange of Personal Data

Date I sent personal data: _____     Date I received personal data: _____

Address: _____     City: _____ State: _____ Zip: _____

Age: _____     Height: _____     Other: _____

Contact Numbers:     Home: _____     Mobile: _____     Other: _____

E-mail address:

## Photo Overview

Photo ☐ Yes / ☐ No

_____
_____

## Let the Journey Begin—Number of Correspondence

| ̶L̶H̶T II | Sent to contact | ̶L̶H̶T II | Received from contact |
|---|---|---|---|
| | E-mail messages | | E-mail messages |
| | Emoticons (winks, smiles, etc.) | | Emoticons (winks, smiles, etc.) |
| | Phone calls | | Phone calls |
| | Virtual dates initiated | | Virtual dates initiated |
| | Live dates initiated | | Live dates initiated |
| | U.S. mail | | U.S. mail |
| | Other | | Other |

## Miscellaneous

_____
_____
_____

# The Online Journey II

Initial thought of profile:
_____

Initial thought of correspondence:
_____

What I like most:
_____

What I like least:
_____

## Comments

Document key information that you want to remember.
*(i.e., great conversationalist, cried on first date, great voice, member looking for long-term relationship, etc.)*

_____
_____
_____
_____
_____
_____
_____
_____
_____

## Blocked Member Details

Date: _____    Blocking Method: _____

Reasons/Details:
_____
_____
_____

Virtual Date:
An event between two individuals
utilizing technology, creativity, and
imagination.

Try it. You'll definitely like it.

~ See chapter 8

Have you met that special one?

# The Online Journey I

## Contact Data

Screen Name: _____ Legal Name: _____

Online Dating Service: _____ Date contact initiated: _____

☐ I initiated contact     ☐ He/She initiated contact

The reason I made contact or responded to contact:

_____

## Exchange of Personal Data

Date I sent personal data: _____ Date I received personal data: _____

Address: _____ City: _____ State: _____ Zip: _____

Age: _____ Height: _____ Other: _____

Contact Numbers:    Home: _____ Mobile: _____ Other: _____

E-mail address:

### Photo Overview

Photo ☐ Yes / ☐ No

_____
_____

## Let the Journey Begin—Number of Correspondence

| ~~IIII~~ II | Sent to contact | ~~IIII~~ II | Received from contact |
|---|---|---|---|
| | E-mail messages | | E-mail messages |
| | Emoticons (winks, smiles, etc.) | | Emoticons (winks, smiles, etc.) |
| | Phone calls | | Phone calls |
| | Virtual dates initiated | | Virtual dates initiated |
| | Live dates initiated | | Live dates initiated |
| | U.S. mail | | U.S. mail |
| | Other | | Other |

## Miscellaneous

_____
_____
_____

# The Online Journey II

Initial thought of profile:
_____

Initial thought of correspondence:
_____

What I like most:
_____

What I like least:
_____

## Comments

Document key information that you want to remember.
*(i.e., great conversationalist, cried on first date, great voice, member looking for long-term relationship, etc.)*

_____
_____
_____
_____
_____
_____
_____
_____
_____
_____

## Blocked Member Details

Date: _____  Blocking Method: _____

Reasons/Details:
_____
_____
_____

# The Online Journey I

## Contact Data

Screen Name: _____ Legal Name: _____

Online Dating Service: _____ Date contact initiated: _____

☐ I initiated contact    ☐ He/She initiated contact

The reason I made contact or responded to contact:

_____

## Exchange of Personal Data

Date I sent personal data: _____ Date I received personal data: _____

Address: _____ City: _____ State: _____ Zip: _____

Age: _____ Height: _____ Other: _____

Contact Numbers:  Home: _____ Mobile: _____ Other: _____

E-mail address:

## Photo Overview

Photo ☐ Yes / ☐ No

_____

_____

## Let the Journey Begin—Number of Correspondence

| ЦНТ ll | Sent to contact | ЦНТ ll | Received from contact |
|---|---|---|---|
| | E-mail messages | | E-mail messages |
| | Emoticons (winks, smiles, etc.) | | Emoticons (winks, smiles, etc.) |
| | Phone calls | | Phone calls |
| | Virtual dates initiated | | Virtual dates initiated |
| | Live dates initiated | | Live dates initiated |
| | U.S. mail | | U.S. mail |
| | Other | | Other |

## Miscellaneous

_____

_____

_____

# The Online Journey II

Member Rating: 1 2 3 4 5 6 7 8 9 10 / ☺ ☺ ☹

Initial thought of profile:
_____

Initial thought of correspondence:
_____

What I like most:
_____

What I like least:
_____

## Comments

Document key information that you want to remember.
*(i.e., great conversationalist, cried on first date, great voice, member looking for long-term relationship, etc.)*

_____
_____
_____
_____
_____
_____
_____
_____
_____

## Blocked Member Details

Date: _____    Blocking Method: _____

Reasons/Details:
_____
_____
_____

# The Online Journey I

## Contact Data

Screen Name: _____    Legal Name: _____

Online Dating Service: _____    Date contact initiated: _____

☐ I initiated contact     ☐ He/She initiated contact

The reason I made contact or responded to contact:

_____

## Exchange of Personal Data

Date I sent personal data: _____    Date I received personal data: _____

Address: _____    City: _____ State: _____ Zip: _____

Age: _____   Height: _____    Other: _____

Contact Numbers:   Home: _____    Mobile: _____ Other: _____

E-mail address:

## Photo Overview

Photo ☐ Yes / ☐ No

_____

_____

## Let the Journey Begin—Number of Correspondence

| ~~IIII~~ II | Sent to contact | ~~IIII~~ II | Received from contact |
|---|---|---|---|
| | E-mail messages | | E-mail messages |
| | Emoticons (winks, smiles, etc.) | | Emoticons (winks, smiles, etc.) |
| | Phone calls | | Phone calls |
| | Virtual dates initiated | | Virtual dates initiated |
| | Live dates initiated | | Live dates initiated |
| | U.S. mail | | U.S. mail |
| | Other | | Other |

## Miscellaneous

_____

_____

_____

# The Online Journey II

Member Rating: 1 2 3 4 5 6 7 8 9 10 / ☺ 😐 ☹

Initial thought of profile:
_____

Initial thought of correspondence:
_____

What I like most:
_____

What I like least:
_____

## Comments

Document key information that you want to remember.
*(i.e., great conversationalist, cried on first date, great voice, member looking for long-term relationship, etc.)*

_____
_____
_____
_____
_____
_____
_____
_____
_____

## Blocked Member Details

Date: _____    Blocking Method: _____

Reasons/Details:
_____
_____
_____

# The Online Journey I

## Contact Data

Screen Name: _____     Legal Name: _____

Online Dating Service: _____     Date contact initiated: _____

☐ I initiated contact     ☐ He/She initiated contact

The reason I made contact or responded to contact:

_____

## Exchange of Personal Data

Date I sent personal data: _____     Date I received personal data: _____

Address: _____     City: _____   State: _____   Zip: _____

Age: _____     Height: _____     Other: _____

Contact Numbers:     Home: _____     Mobile: _____   Other: _____

E-mail address:

## Photo Overview

Photo ☐ Yes / ☐ No

_____

_____

## Let the Journey Begin—Number of Correspondence

| ̶|̶|̶|̶ || | Sent to contact | ̶|̶|̶|̶ || | Received from contact |
|---|---|---|---|
| | E-mail messages | | E-mail messages |
| | Emoticons (winks, smiles, etc.) | | Emoticons (winks, smiles, etc.) |
| | Phone calls | | Phone calls |
| | Virtual dates initiated | | Virtual dates initiated |
| | Live dates initiated | | Live dates initiated |
| | U.S. mail | | U.S. mail |
| | Other | | Other |

## Miscellaneous

_____

_____

_____

# The Online Journey II

Member Rating: 1 2 3 4 5 6 7 8 9 10 / ☺ ☺ ☹

Initial thought of profile:

_____

Initial thought of correspondence:

_____

What I like most:

_____

What I like least:

_____

## Comments

Document key information that you want to remember.
*(i.e., great conversationalist, cried on first date, great voice, member looking for long-term relationship, etc.)*

_____
_____
_____
_____
_____
_____
_____
_____
_____
_____

## Blocked Member Details

Date: _____    Blocking Method: _____

Reasons/Details:

_____
_____
_____

# The Online Journey I

## Contact Data

Screen Name: _____     Legal Name: _____

Online Dating Service: _____     Date contact initiated: _____

☐ I initiated contact     ☐ He/She initiated contact

The reason I made contact or responded to contact:

_____

## Exchange of Personal Data

Date I sent personal data: _____     Date I received personal data: _____

Address: _____     City: _____   State: _____   Zip: _____

Age: _____    Height: _____    Other: _____

Contact Numbers:   Home: _____    Mobile: _____    Other: _____

E-mail address:

## Photo Overview

Photo ☐ Yes / ☐ No

_____

_____

## Let the Journey Begin—Number of Correspondence

| ̶H̶T̶ II | Sent to contact | ̶H̶T̶ II | Received from contact |
|---|---|---|---|
| | E-mail messages | | E-mail messages |
| | Emoticons (winks, smiles, etc.) | | Emoticons (winks, smiles, etc.) |
| | Phone calls | | Phone calls |
| | Virtual dates initiated | | Virtual dates initiated |
| | Live dates initiated | | Live dates initiated |
| | U.S. mail | | U.S. mail |
| | Other | | Other |

## Miscellaneous

_____

_____

_____

# The Online Journey II

Initial thought of profile:
_____

Initial thought of correspondence:
_____

What I like most:
_____

What I like least:
_____

## Comments

Document key information that you want to remember.
*(i.e., great conversationalist, cried on first date, great voice, member looking for long-term relationship, etc.)*

_____
_____
_____
_____
_____
_____
_____
_____
_____

## Blocked Member Details

Date: _____ Blocking Method: _____

Reasons/Details:
_____
_____
_____

# The Online Journey I

## Contact Data

Screen Name: _____     Legal Name: _____

Online Dating Service: _____     Date contact initiated: _____

☐ I initiated contact     ☐ He/She initiated contact

The reason I made contact or responded to contact:

_____

## Exchange of Personal Data

Date I sent personal data: _____     Date I received personal data: _____

Address: _____     City: _____ State: _____ Zip: _____

Age: _____     Height: _____     Other: _____

Contact Numbers:     Home: _____     Mobile: _____     Other: _____

E-mail address:

## Photo Overview

Photo ☐ Yes / ☐ No

_____

_____

## Let the Journey Begin—Number of Correspondence

| ~~|||~~ || | Sent to contact | ~~|||~~ || | Received from contact |
|---|---|---|---|
| | E-mail messages | | E-mail messages |
| | Emoticons (winks, smiles, etc.) | | Emoticons (winks, smiles, etc.) |
| | Phone calls | | Phone calls |
| | Virtual dates initiated | | Virtual dates initiated |
| | Live dates initiated | | Live dates initiated |
| | U.S. mail | | U.S. mail |
| | Other | | Other |

## Miscellaneous

_____

_____

_____

# The Online Journey II

Initial thought of profile:
_____

Initial thought of correspondence:
_____

What I like most:
_____

What I like least:
_____

## Comments

Document key information that you want to remember.
*(i.e., great conversationalist, cried on first date, great voice, member looking for long-term relationship, etc.)*

_____
_____
_____
_____
_____
_____
_____
_____
_____
_____

## Blocked Member Details

Date: _____  Blocking Method: _____

Reasons/Details:
_____
_____
_____

*Finding virtue takes patience.*

# The Online Journey I

## Contact Data

Screen Name: _____     Legal Name: _____

Online Dating Service: _____     Date contact initiated: _____

☐ I initiated contact     ☐ He/She initiated contact

The reason I made contact or responded to contact:

_____

## Exchange of Personal Data

Date I sent personal data: _____     Date I received personal data: _____

Address: _____     City: _____  State: _____  Zip: _____

Age: _____     Height: _____     Other: _____

Contact Numbers:     Home: _____     Mobile: _____  Other: _____

E-mail address:

### Photo Overview

Photo ☐ Yes / ☐ No

_____
_____

## Let the Journey Begin—Number of Correspondence

| ~~IIII~~ II | Sent to contact | ~~IIII~~ II | Received from contact |
|---|---|---|---|
| | E-mail messages | | E-mail messages |
| | Emoticons (winks, smiles, etc.) | | Emoticons (winks, smiles, etc.) |
| | Phone calls | | Phone calls |
| | Virtual dates initiated | | Virtual dates initiated |
| | Live dates initiated | | Live dates initiated |
| | U.S. mail | | U.S. mail |
| | Other | | Other |

## Miscellaneous

_____
_____
_____

# The Online Journey II

Member Rating: 1 2 3 4 5 6 7 8 9 10 / ☺ ☺ ☹

Initial thought of profile:
_____

Initial thought of correspondence:
_____

What I like most:
_____

What I like least:
_____

## Comments

Document key information that you want to remember.
*(i.e., great conversationalist, cried on first date, great voice, member looking for long-term relationship, etc.)*

_____
_____
_____
_____
_____
_____
_____
_____
_____

## Blocked Member Details

Date: _____    Blocking Method: _____

Reasons/Details:
_____
_____
_____

# The Online Journey I

## Contact Data

Screen Name: _____     Legal Name: _____

Online Dating Service: _____     Date contact initiated: _____

☐ I initiated contact      ☐ He/She initiated contact

The reason I made contact or responded to contact:

_____

## Exchange of Personal Data

Date I sent personal data: _____     Date I received personal data: _____

Address: _____     City: _____  State: _____  Zip: _____

Age: _____     Height: _____     Other: _____

Contact Numbers:    Home: _____     Mobile: _____  Other: _____

E-mail address:

## Photo Overview

Photo ☐ Yes / ☐ No

_____

_____

## Let the Journey Begin—Number of Correspondence

| ͰͰͰ ΙΙ | Sent to contact | ͰͰͰ ΙΙ | Received from contact |
|---|---|---|---|
|  | E-mail messages |  | E-mail messages |
|  | Emoticons (winks, smiles, etc.) |  | Emoticons (winks, smiles, etc.) |
|  | Phone calls |  | Phone calls |
|  | Virtual dates initiated |  | Virtual dates initiated |
|  | Live dates initiated |  | Live dates initiated |
|  | U.S. mail |  | U.S. mail |
|  | Other |  | Other |

## Miscellaneous

_____

_____

_____

# The Online Journey II

Member Rating: 1 2 3 4 5 6 7 8 9 10 / ☺ ☺ ☹

Initial thought of profile:

_____

Initial thought of correspondence:

_____

What I like most:

_____

What I like least:

_____

## Comments

Document key information that you want to remember.
*(i.e., great conversationalist, cried on first date, great voice, member looking for long-term relationship, etc.)*

_____
_____
_____
_____
_____
_____
_____
_____
_____
_____

## Blocked Member Details

Date: _____    Blocking Method: _____

Reasons/Details:

_____
_____
_____

# The Online Journey I

## Contact Data

Screen Name: _____     Legal Name: _____

Online Dating Service: _____     Date contact initiated: _____

☐ I initiated contact     ☐ He/She initiated contact

The reason I made contact or responded to contact:

_____

## Exchange of Personal Data

Date I sent personal data: _____     Date I received personal data: _____

Address: _____     City: _____ State: _____ Zip: _____

Age: _____     Height: _____     Other: _____

Contact Numbers:     Home: _____     Mobile: _____ Other: _____

E-mail address:

## Photo Overview

Photo ☐ Yes / ☐ No

_____
_____

## Let the Journey Begin—Number of Correspondence

| ̶I̶I̶I̶I̶ II | Sent to contact | ̶I̶I̶I̶I̶ II | Received from contact |
|---|---|---|---|
| | E-mail messages | | E-mail messages |
| | Emoticons (winks, smiles, etc.) | | Emoticons (winks, smiles, etc.) |
| | Phone calls | | Phone calls |
| | Virtual dates initiated | | Virtual dates initiated |
| | Live dates initiated | | Live dates initiated |
| | U.S. mail | | U.S. mail |
| | Other | | Other |

## Miscellaneous

_____
_____
_____

# The Online Journey II

Member Rating: 1 2 3 4 5 6 7 8 9 10 / ☺ ☺ ☹

Initial thought of profile:

_____

Initial thought of correspondence:

_____

What I like most:

_____

What I like least:

_____

## Comments
Document key information that you want to remember.
*(i.e., great conversationalist, cried on first date, great voice, member looking for long-term relationship, etc.)*

_____
_____
_____
_____
_____
_____
_____
_____
_____
_____

## Blocked Member Details

Date: _____  Blocking Method: _____

Reasons/Details:

_____
_____
_____

# The Online Journey I

## Contact Data

Screen Name: _____     Legal Name: _____

Online Dating Service: _____     Date contact initiated: _____

☐ I initiated contact     ☐ He/She initiated contact

The reason I made contact or responded to contact:

_____

## Exchange of Personal Data

Date I sent personal data: _____     Date I received personal data: _____

Address: _____     City: _____  State: _____  Zip: _____

Age: _____     Height: _____     Other: _____

Contact Numbers:     Home: _____     Mobile: _____     Other: _____

E-mail address:

## Photo Overview

Photo ☐ Yes / ☐ No

_____

_____

## Let the Journey Begin—Number of Correspondence

| ̶I̶H̶T̶ ̶I̶I̶ | Sent to contact | ̶I̶H̶T̶ ̶I̶I̶ | Received from contact |
|---|---|---|---|
| | E-mail messages | | E-mail messages |
| | Emoticons (winks, smiles, etc.) | | Emoticons (winks, smiles, etc.) |
| | Phone calls | | Phone calls |
| | Virtual dates initiated | | Virtual dates initiated |
| | Live dates initiated | | Live dates initiated |
| | U.S. mail | | U.S. mail |
| | Other | | Other |

## Miscellaneous

_____

_____

_____

# The Online Journey II

**Member Rating:** 1 2 3 4 5 6 7 8 9 10 / ☺ ☻ ☹

Initial thought of profile:

_____

Initial thought of correspondence:

_____

What I like most:

_____

What I like least:

_____

## Comments

Document key information that you want to remember.
*(i.e., great conversationalist, cried on first date, great voice, member looking for long-term relationship, etc.)*

_____
_____
_____
_____
_____
_____
_____
_____
_____
_____

## Blocked Member Details

Date: _____    Blocking Method: _____

Reasons/Details:

_____
_____
_____

# The Online Journey I

## Contact Data

Screen Name: _____          Legal Name: _____

Online Dating Service: _____          Date contact initiated: _____

☐ I initiated contact          ☐ He/She initiated contact

The reason I made contact or responded to contact:

_____

## Exchange of Personal Data

Date I sent personal data: _____          Date I received personal data: _____

Address: _____          City: _____  State: _____  Zip: _____

Age: _____          Height: _____          Other: _____

Contact Numbers:     Home: _____          Mobile: _____     Other: _____

E-mail address:

## Photo Overview

Photo ☐ Yes / ☐ No

_____

_____

## Let the Journey Begin—Number of Correspondence

| ~~IIII~~ II | Sent to contact | ~~IIII~~ II | Received from contact |
|---|---|---|---|
| | E-mail messages | | E-mail messages |
| | Emoticons (winks, smiles, etc.) | | Emoticons (winks, smiles, etc.) |
| | Phone calls | | Phone calls |
| | Virtual dates initiated | | Virtual dates initiated |
| | Live dates initiated | | Live dates initiated |
| | U.S. mail | | U.S. mail |
| | Other | | Other |

## Miscellaneous

_____

_____

_____

# The Online Journey II

Initial thought of profile:

_____

Initial thought of correspondence:

_____

What I like most:

_____

What I like least:

_____

## Comments

Document key information that you want to remember.
*(i.e., great conversationalist, cried on first date, great voice, member looking for long-term relationship, etc.)*

_____
_____
_____
_____
_____
_____
_____
_____
_____
_____

## Blocked Member Details

Date: _____   Blocking Method: _____

Reasons/Details:

_____
_____
_____

*Want to see beauty? Find a mirror.*

# The Online Journey I

## Contact Data

Screen Name: _____    Legal Name: _____

Online Dating Service: _____    Date contact initiated: _____

☐ I initiated contact    ☐ He/She initiated contact

The reason I made contact or responded to contact:

_____

## Exchange of Personal Data

Date I sent personal data: _____    Date I received personal data: _____

Address: _____    City: _____ State: _____ Zip: _____

Age: _____    Height: _____    Other: _____

Contact Numbers:    Home: _____    Mobile: _____ Other: _____

E-mail address:

## Photo Overview

Photo ☐ Yes / ☐ No

_____

_____

## Let the Journey Begin—Number of Correspondence

| ǁ̶H̶ ǁ | Sent to contact | ǁ̶H̶ ǁ | Received from contact |
|---|---|---|---|
| | E-mail messages | | E-mail messages |
| | Emoticons (winks, smiles, etc.) | | Emoticons (winks, smiles, etc.) |
| | Phone calls | | Phone calls |
| | Virtual dates initiated | | Virtual dates initiated |
| | Live dates initiated | | Live dates initiated |
| | U.S. mail | | U.S. mail |
| | Other | | Other |

## Miscellaneous

_____

_____

_____

# The Online Journey II

Member Rating: 1 2 3 4 5 6 7 8 9 10 / ☺ ☺ ☹

Initial thought of profile:
_____

Initial thought of correspondence:
_____

What I like most:
_____

What I like least:
_____

## Comments
### Document key information that you want to remember.
*(i.e., great conversationalist, cried on first date, great voice, member looking for long-term relationship, etc.)*

_____
_____
_____
_____
_____
_____
_____
_____
_____
_____

## Blocked Member Details

Date: _____    Blocking Method: _____

Reasons/Details:
_____
_____
_____

# The Online Journey I

## Contact Data

Screen Name: _____    Legal Name: _____

Online Dating Service: _____    Date contact initiated: _____

☐ I initiated contact     ☐ He/She initiated contact

The reason I made contact or responded to contact:

_____

## Exchange of Personal Data

Date I sent personal data: _____    Date I received personal data: _____

Address: _____    City: _____    State: _____    Zip: _____

Age: _____    Height: _____    Other: _____

Contact Numbers:    Home: _____    Mobile: _____    Other: _____

E-mail address:

## Photo Overview

Photo ☐ Yes / ☐ No

_____

_____

## Let the Journey Begin—Number of Correspondence

| ɪɪɪɪ ɪɪ | Sent to contact | ɪɪɪɪ ɪɪ | Received from contact |
|---|---|---|---|
| | E-mail messages | | E-mail messages |
| | Emoticons (winks, smiles, etc.) | | Emoticons (winks, smiles, etc.) |
| | Phone calls | | Phone calls |
| | Virtual dates initiated | | Virtual dates initiated |
| | Live dates initiated | | Live dates initiated |
| | U.S. mail | | U.S. mail |
| | Other | | Other |

## Miscellaneous

_____

_____

_____

# The Online Journey II

Member Rating: 1 2 3 4 5 6 7 8 9 10 / ☺ ☻ ☹

Initial thought of profile:
_____

Initial thought of correspondence:
_____

What I like most:
_____

What I like least:
_____

## Comments

Document key information that you want to remember.
*(i.e., great conversationalist, cried on first date, great voice, member looking for long-term relationship, etc.)*

_____
_____
_____
_____
_____
_____
_____
_____
_____

## Blocked Member Details

Date: _____     Blocking Method: _____

Reasons/Details:
_____
_____
_____

# The Online Journey I

## Contact Data

Screen Name: _____    Legal Name: _____

Online Dating Service: _____    Date contact initiated: _____

☐ I initiated contact     ☐ He/She initiated contact

The reason I made contact or responded to contact:

_____

## Exchange of Personal Data

Date I sent personal data: _____    Date I received personal data: _____

Address: _____    City: _____ State: _____ Zip: _____

Age: _____    Height: _____    Other: _____

Contact Numbers:   Home: _____    Mobile: _____    Other: _____

E-mail address:

## Photo Overview

Photo ☐ Yes / ☐ No

_____

_____

## Let the Journey Begin—Number of Correspondence

| ~~IIII~~ II | Sent to contact | ~~IIII~~ II | Received from contact |
|---|---|---|---|
| | E-mail messages | | E-mail messages |
| | Emoticons (winks, smiles, etc.) | | Emoticons (winks, smiles, etc.) |
| | Phone calls | | Phone calls |
| | Virtual dates initiated | | Virtual dates initiated |
| | Live dates initiated | | Live dates initiated |
| | U.S. mail | | U.S. mail |
| | Other | | Other |

## Miscellaneous

_____

_____

_____

# The Online Journey II

Initial thought of profile:
_____

Initial thought of correspondence:
_____

What I like most:
_____

What I like least:
_____

## Comments

Document key information that you want to remember.
*(i.e., great conversationalist, cried on first date, great voice, member looking for long-term relationship, etc.)*

_____
_____
_____
_____
_____
_____
_____
_____
_____
_____

## Blocked Member Details

Date: _____     Blocking Method: _____

Reasons/Details:
_____
_____
_____

# The Online Journey I

## Contact Data

Screen Name: _____    Legal Name: _____

Online Dating Service: _____    Date contact initiated: _____

☐ I initiated contact    ☐ He/She initiated contact

The reason I made contact or responded to contact:

_____

## Exchange of Personal Data

Date I sent personal data: _____    Date I received personal data: _____

Address: _____    City: _____    State: _____    Zip: _____

Age: _____    Height: _____    Other: _____

Contact Numbers:    Home: _____    Mobile: _____    Other: _____

E-mail address:

### Photo Overview

Photo ☐ Yes / ☐ No

_____

_____

## Let the Journey Begin—Number of Correspondence

| ⊮ ‖ | Sent to contact | ⊮ ‖ | Received from contact |
|---|---|---|---|
| | E-mail messages | | E-mail messages |
| | Emoticons (winks, smiles, etc.) | | Emoticons (winks, smiles, etc.) |
| | Phone calls | | Phone calls |
| | Virtual dates initiated | | Virtual dates initiated |
| | Live dates initiated | | Live dates initiated |
| | U.S. mail | | U.S. mail |
| | Other | | Other |

## Miscellaneous

_____

_____

_____

# The Online Journey II

Initial thought of profile:
_____

Initial thought of correspondence:
_____

What I like most:
_____

What I like least:
_____

## Comments

Document key information that you want to remember.
*(i.e., great conversationalist, cried on first date, great voice, member looking for long-term relationship, etc.)*

_____
_____
_____
_____
_____
_____
_____
_____
_____
_____

## Blocked Member Details

Date: _____    Blocking Method: _____

Reasons/Details:
_____
_____
_____

# The Online Journey I

## Contact Data

Screen Name: _____     Legal Name: _____

Online Dating Service: _____     Date contact initiated: _____

☐ I initiated contact     ☐ He/She initiated contact

The reason I made contact or responded to contact:

_____

## Exchange of Personal Data

Date I sent personal data: _____     Date I received personal data: _____

Address: _____     City: _____ State: _____ Zip: _____

Age: _____    Height: _____    Other: _____

Contact Numbers:   Home: _____    Mobile: _____    Other: _____

E-mail address:

## Photo Overview

Photo ☐ Yes / ☐ No

_____

_____

## Let the Journey Begin—Number of Correspondence

| ~~lllll~~ ll | Sent to contact | ~~lllll~~ ll | Received from contact |
|---|---|---|---|
| | E-mail messages | | E-mail messages |
| | Emoticons (winks, smiles, etc.) | | Emoticons (winks, smiles, etc.) |
| | Phone calls | | Phone calls |
| | Virtual dates initiated | | Virtual dates initiated |
| | Live dates initiated | | Live dates initiated |
| | U.S. mail | | U.S. mail |
| | Other | | Other |

## Miscellaneous

_____

_____

_____

# The Online Journey II

Initial thought of profile:
_____

Initial thought of correspondence:
_____

What I like most:
_____

What I like least:
_____

## Comments

Document key information that you want to remember.
*(i.e., great conversationalist, cried on first date, great voice, member looking for long-term relationship, etc.)*

_____
_____
_____
_____
_____
_____
_____
_____
_____

## Blocked Member Details

Date: _____     Blocking Method: _____

Reasons/Details:
_____
_____
_____

*First, love yourself.*

# The Online Journey I

## Contact Data

Screen Name: _____    Legal Name: _____

Online Dating Service: _____    Date contact initiated: _____

☐ I initiated contact    ☐ He/She initiated contact

The reason I made contact or responded to contact:

_____

## Exchange of Personal Data

Date I sent personal data: _____    Date I received personal data: _____

Address: _____    City: _____    State: _____    Zip: _____

Age: _____    Height: _____    Other: _____

Contact Numbers:    Home: _____    Mobile: _____    Other: _____

E-mail address:

## Photo Overview

Photo ☐ Yes / ☐ No

_____

_____

## Let the Journey Begin—Number of Correspondence

| ~~IIII~~ II | Sent to contact | ~~IIII~~ II | Received from contact |
|---|---|---|---|
| | E-mail messages | | E-mail messages |
| | Emoticons (winks, smiles, etc.) | | Emoticons (winks, smiles, etc.) |
| | Phone calls | | Phone calls |
| | Virtual dates initiated | | Virtual dates initiated |
| | Live dates initiated | | Live dates initiated |
| | U.S. mail | | U.S. mail |
| | Other | | Other |

## Miscellaneous

_____

_____

_____

# The Online Journey II

Initial thought of profile:
_____

Initial thought of correspondence:
_____

What I like most:
_____

What I like least:
_____

## Comments

Document key information that you want to remember.
*(i.e., great conversationalist, cried on first date, great voice, member looking for long-term relationship, etc.)*

_____
_____
_____
_____
_____
_____
_____
_____
_____
_____

## Blocked Member Details

Date: _____    Blocking Method: _____

Reasons/Details:
_____
_____
_____

# The Online Journey I

## Contact Data

Screen Name: _____  Legal Name: _____

Online Dating Service: _____  Date contact initiated: _____

☐ I initiated contact    ☐ He/She initiated contact

The reason I made contact or responded to contact:

_____

## Exchange of Personal Data

Date I sent personal data: _____  Date I received personal data: _____

Address: _____  City: _____  State: _____  Zip: _____

Age: _____  Height: _____  Other: _____

Contact Numbers:  Home: _____  Mobile: _____  Other: _____

E-mail address:

## Photo Overview

Photo ☐ Yes / ☐ No

_____
_____

## Let the Journey Begin—Number of Correspondence

| ЛНΤ ΙΙ | Sent to contact | ЛНΤ ΙΙ | Received from contact |
|---|---|---|---|
| | E-mail messages | | E-mail messages |
| | Emoticons (winks, smiles, etc.) | | Emoticons (winks, smiles, etc.) |
| | Phone calls | | Phone calls |
| | Virtual dates initiated | | Virtual dates initiated |
| | Live dates initiated | | Live dates initiated |
| | U.S. mail | | U.S. mail |
| | Other | | Other |

## Miscellaneous

_____
_____
_____

# The Online Journey II

Initial thought of profile:

_____

Initial thought of correspondence:

_____

What I like most:

_____

What I like least:

_____

## Comments

Document key information that you want to remember.
*(i.e., great conversationalist, cried on first date, great voice, member looking for long-term relationship, etc.)*

_____
_____
_____
_____
_____
_____
_____
_____
_____

## Blocked Member Details

Date: _____ Blocking Method: _____

Reasons/Details:

_____
_____
_____

# The Online Journey I

## Contact Data

Screen Name: _____  Legal Name: _____

Online Dating Service: _____  Date contact initiated: _____

☐ I initiated contact     ☐ He/She initiated contact

The reason I made contact or responded to contact:

_____

## Exchange of Personal Data

Date I sent personal data: _____   Date I received personal data: _____

Address: _____   City: _____  State: _____  Zip: _____

Age: _____   Height: _____   Other: _____

Contact Numbers:   Home: _____   Mobile: _____   Other: _____

E-mail address:

## Photo Overview

Photo ☐ Yes / ☐ No

_____
_____

## Let the Journey Begin—Number of Correspondence

| ~~|||| ~~ || | Sent to contact | ~~|||| ~~ || | Received from contact |
|---|---|---|---|
| | E-mail messages | | E-mail messages |
| | Emoticons (winks, smiles, etc.) | | Emoticons (winks, smiles, etc.) |
| | Phone calls | | Phone calls |
| | Virtual dates initiated | | Virtual dates initiated |
| | Live dates initiated | | Live dates initiated |
| | U.S. mail | | U.S. mail |
| | Other | | Other |

## Miscellaneous

_____
_____
_____

# The Online Journey II

Initial thought of profile:

_____

Initial thought of correspondence:

_____

What I like most:

_____

What I like least:

_____

## Comments

Document key information that you want to remember.
*(i.e., great conversationalist, cried on first date, great voice, member looking for long-term relationship, etc.)*

_____
_____
_____
_____
_____
_____
_____
_____
_____
_____

## Blocked Member Details

Date: _____    Blocking Method: _____

Reasons/Details:

_____
_____
_____

# The Online Journey I

## Contact Data

Screen Name: _____     Legal Name: _____

Online Dating Service: _____     Date contact initiated: _____

☐ I initiated contact     ☐ He/She initiated contact

The reason I made contact or responded to contact:

_____

## Exchange of Personal Data

Date I sent personal data: _____     Date I received personal data: _____

Address: _____     City: _____     State: _____     Zip: _____

Age: _____     Height: _____     Other: _____

Contact Numbers:     Home: _____     Mobile: _____     Other: _____

E-mail address:

## Photo Overview

Photo ☐ Yes / ☐ No

_____

_____

## Let the Journey Begin—Number of Correspondence

| ~~IIII~~ II | Sent to contact | ~~IIII~~ II | Received from contact |
|---|---|---|---|
| | E-mail messages | | E-mail messages |
| | Emoticons (winks, smiles, etc.) | | Emoticons (winks, smiles, etc.) |
| | Phone calls | | Phone calls |
| | Virtual dates initiated | | Virtual dates initiated |
| | Live dates initiated | | Live dates initiated |
| | U.S. mail | | U.S. mail |
| | Other | | Other |

## Miscellaneous

_____

_____

_____

# The Online Journey II

Initial thought of profile:

_____

Initial thought of correspondence:

_____

What I like most:

_____

What I like least:

_____

## Comments

Document key information that you want to remember.
*(i.e., great conversationalist, cried on first date, great voice, member looking for long-term relationship, etc.)*

_____
_____
_____
_____
_____
_____
_____
_____
_____

## Blocked Member Details

Date: _____    Blocking Method: _____

Reasons/Details:

_____
_____
_____

How long has it been since
you updated your profile?

List the items that you plan to update on your online profile.

_____

_____

_____

_____

_____

_____

_____

# The Online Journey I

## Contact Data

Screen Name: _____    Legal Name: _____

Online Dating Service: _____    Date contact initiated: _____

☐ I initiated contact    ☐ He/She initiated contact

The reason I made contact or responded to contact:

_____

## Exchange of Personal Data

Date I sent personal data: _____    Date I received personal data: _____

Address: _____    City: _____ State: _____ Zip: _____

Age: _____    Height: _____    Other: _____

Contact Numbers:    Home: _____    Mobile: _____    Other: _____

E-mail address:

### Photo Overview

Photo ☐ Yes / ☐ No

_____
_____

## Let the Journey Begin—Number of Correspondence

| ||| || | Sent to contact | ||| || | Received from contact |
|---|---|---|---|
| | E-mail messages | | E-mail messages |
| | Emoticons (winks, smiles, etc.) | | Emoticons (winks, smiles, etc.) |
| | Phone calls | | Phone calls |
| | Virtual dates initiated | | Virtual dates initiated |
| | Live dates initiated | | Live dates initiated |
| | U.S. mail | | U.S. mail |
| | Other | | Other |

## Miscellaneous

_____
_____
_____

# The Online Journey II

Initial thought of profile:

_____

Initial thought of correspondence:

_____

What I like most:

_____

What I like least:

_____

## Comments

Document key information that you want to remember.
*(i.e., great conversationalist, cried on first date, great voice, member looking for long-term relationship, etc.)*

_____
_____
_____
_____
_____
_____
_____
_____
_____

## Blocked Member Details

Date: _____ Blocking Method: _____

Reasons/Details:

_____
_____
_____

*Laugh until you gasp for breath.*

# The Online Journey I

## Contact Data

Screen Name: _____  Legal Name: _____

Online Dating Service: _____  Date contact initiated: _____

☐ I initiated contact    ☐ He/She initiated contact

The reason I made contact or responded to contact:

_____

## Exchange of Personal Data

Date I sent personal data: _____  Date I received personal data: _____

Address: _____  City: _____ State: _____ Zip: _____

Age: _____  Height: _____  Other: _____

Contact Numbers:  Home: _____  Mobile: _____ Other: _____

E-mail address:

### Photo Overview

Photo ☐ Yes / ☐ No

_____
_____

## Let the Journey Begin—Number of Correspondence

| ʜʜ‖ | Sent to contact | ʜʜ‖ | Received from contact |
|---|---|---|---|
| | E-mail messages | | E-mail messages |
| | Emoticons (winks, smiles, etc.) | | Emoticons (winks, smiles, etc.) |
| | Phone calls | | Phone calls |
| | Virtual dates initiated | | Virtual dates initiated |
| | Live dates initiated | | Live dates initiated |
| | U.S. mail | | U.S. mail |
| | Other | | Other |

## Miscellaneous

_____
_____
_____

# The Online Journey II

Member Rating: 1 2 3 4 5 6 7 8 9 10 / ☺ ☺ ☹

Initial thought of profile:
_____

Initial thought of correspondence:
_____

What I like most:
_____

What I like least:
_____

## Comments

Document key information that you want to remember.
*(i.e., great conversationalist, cried on first date, great voice, member looking for long-term relationship, etc.)*

_____
_____
_____
_____
_____
_____
_____
_____
_____

## Blocked Member Details

Date: _____     Blocking Method: _____

Reasons/Details:
_____
_____
_____

# The Online Journey I

## Contact Data

Screen Name: _____  Legal Name: _____

Online Dating Service: _____  Date contact initiated: _____

☐ I initiated contact   ☐ He/She initiated contact

The reason I made contact or responded to contact:

_____

## Exchange of Personal Data

Date I sent personal data: _____  Date I received personal data: _____

Address: _____  City: _____  State: _____  Zip: _____

Age: _____  Height: _____  Other: _____

Contact Numbers:  Home: _____  Mobile: _____  Other: _____

E-mail address:

## Photo Overview

Photo ☐ Yes / ☐ No

_____

_____

## Let the Journey Begin—Number of Correspondence

| JHT II | Sent to contact | JHT II | Received from contact |
|---|---|---|---|
| | E-mail messages | | E-mail messages |
| | Emoticons (winks, smiles, etc.) | | Emoticons (winks, smiles, etc.) |
| | Phone calls | | Phone calls |
| | Virtual dates initiated | | Virtual dates initiated |
| | Live dates initiated | | Live dates initiated |
| | U.S. mail | | U.S. mail |
| | Other | | Other |

## Miscellaneous

_____

_____

_____

# The Online Journey II

Initial thought of profile:

_____

Initial thought of correspondence:

_____

What I like most:

_____

What I like least:

_____

## Comments

Document key information that you want to remember.
*(i.e., great conversationalist, cried on first date, great voice, member looking for long-term relationship, etc.)*

_____
_____
_____
_____
_____
_____
_____
_____
_____

## Blocked Member Details

Date: _____ Blocking Method: _____

Reasons/Details:

_____
_____
_____

# The Online Journey I

## Contact Data

Screen Name: _____     Legal Name: _____

Online Dating Service: _____     Date contact initiated: _____

☐ I initiated contact     ☐ He/She initiated contact

The reason I made contact or responded to contact:

_____

## Exchange of Personal Data

Date I sent personal data: _____     Date I received personal data: _____

Address: _____     City: _____ State: _____ Zip: _____

Age: _____     Height: _____     Other: _____

Contact Numbers:     Home: _____     Mobile: _____ Other: _____

E-mail address:

## Photo Overview

Photo ☐ Yes / ☐ No

_____

_____

## Let the Journey Begin—Number of Correspondence

| ⎢⎢⎢⎢ ⎢⎢ | Sent to contact | ⎢⎢⎢⎢ ⎢⎢ | Received from contact |
|---|---|---|---|
| | E-mail messages | | E-mail messages |
| | Emoticons (winks, smiles, etc.) | | Emoticons (winks, smiles, etc.) |
| | Phone calls | | Phone calls |
| | Virtual dates initiated | | Virtual dates initiated |
| | Live dates initiated | | Live dates initiated |
| | U.S. mail | | U.S. mail |
| | Other | | Other |

## Miscellaneous

_____

_____

_____

# The Online Journey II

Member Rating: 1 2 3 4 5 6 7 8 9 10 / ☺ ☺ ☹

Initial thought of profile:

_____

Initial thought of correspondence:

_____

What I like most:

_____

What I like least:

_____

## Comments

Document key information that you want to remember.
*(i.e., great conversationalist, cried on first date, great voice, member looking for long-term relationship, etc.)*

_____
_____
_____
_____
_____
_____
_____
_____
_____

## Blocked Member Details

Date: _____     Blocking Method: _____

Reasons/Details:

_____
_____
_____

# The Online Journey I

## Contact Data

Screen Name: _____     Legal Name: _____

Online Dating Service: _____     Date contact initiated: _____

☐ I initiated contact     ☐ He/She initiated contact

The reason I made contact or responded to contact:

_____

## Exchange of Personal Data

Date I sent personal data: _____     Date I received personal data: _____

Address: _____     City: _____ State: _____ Zip: _____

Age: _____     Height: _____     Other: _____

Contact Numbers:     Home: _____     Mobile: _____ Other: _____

E-mail address:

## Photo Overview

Photo ☐ Yes / ☐ No

_____

_____

## Let the Journey Begin—Number of Correspondence

| ~~IIII~~ II | Sent to contact | ~~IIII~~ II | Received from contact |
|---|---|---|---|
| | E-mail messages | | E-mail messages |
| | Emoticons (winks, smiles, etc.) | | Emoticons (winks, smiles, etc.) |
| | Phone calls | | Phone calls |
| | Virtual dates initiated | | Virtual dates initiated |
| | Live dates initiated | | Live dates initiated |
| | U.S. mail | | U.S. mail |
| | Other | | Other |

## Miscellaneous

_____

_____

_____

# The Online Journey II

Initial thought of profile:
_____

Initial thought of correspondence:
_____

What I like most:
_____

What I like least:
_____

## Comments

Document key information that you want to remember.
*(i.e., great conversationalist, cried on first date, great voice, member looking for long-term relationship, etc.)*

_____
_____
_____
_____
_____
_____
_____
_____
_____

## Blocked Member Details

Date: _____   Blocking Method: _____

Reasons/Details:
_____
_____
_____

# The Online Journey I

## Contact Data

Screen Name: _____    Legal Name: _____

Online Dating Service: _____    Date contact initiated: _____

☐ I initiated contact    ☐ He/She initiated contact

The reason I made contact or responded to contact:

_____

## Exchange of Personal Data

Date I sent personal data: _____    Date I received personal data: _____

Address: _____    City: _____  State: _____  Zip: _____

Age: _____    Height: _____    Other: _____

Contact Numbers:    Home: _____    Mobile: _____    Other: _____

E-mail address:

## Photo Overview

Photo ☐ Yes / ☐ No

_____

_____

## Let the Journey Begin—Number of Correspondence

| ~~IIII~~ II | Sent to contact | ~~IIII~~ II | Received from contact |
|---|---|---|---|
| | E-mail messages | | E-mail messages |
| | Emoticons (winks, smiles, etc.) | | Emoticons (winks, smiles, etc.) |
| | Phone calls | | Phone calls |
| | Virtual dates initiated | | Virtual dates initiated |
| | Live dates initiated | | Live dates initiated |
| | U.S. mail | | U.S. mail |
| | Other | | Other |

## Miscellaneous

_____

_____

_____

# The Online Journey II

Initial thought of profile:

_____

Initial thought of correspondence:

_____

What I like most:

_____

What I like least:

_____

## Comments
Document key information that you want to remember.
*(i.e., great conversationalist, cried on first date, great voice, member looking for long-term relationship, etc.)*

_____
_____
_____
_____
_____
_____
_____
_____
_____

## Blocked Member Details

Date: _____ Blocking Method: _____

Reasons/Details:

_____
_____
_____

*Take your time; no rush here.*

# The Online Journey I

## Contact Data

Screen Name: _____     Legal Name: _____

Online Dating Service: _____     Date contact initiated: _____

☐ I initiated contact     ☐ He/She initiated contact

The reason I made contact or responded to contact:

_____

## Exchange of Personal Data

Date I sent personal data: _____    Date I received personal data: _____

Address: _____    City: _____ State: _____ Zip: _____

Age: _____    Height: _____    Other: _____

Contact Numbers:   Home: _____    Mobile: _____   Other: _____

E-mail address:

## Photo Overview

Photo ☐ Yes / ☐ No

_____

_____

## Let the Journey Begin—Number of Correspondence

| ɪɪɪɪ ıı | Sent to contact | ɪɪɪɪ ıı | Received from contact |
|---|---|---|---|
| | E-mail messages | | E-mail messages |
| | Emoticons (winks, smiles, etc.) | | Emoticons (winks, smiles, etc.) |
| | Phone calls | | Phone calls |
| | Virtual dates initiated | | Virtual dates initiated |
| | Live dates initiated | | Live dates initiated |
| | U.S. mail | | U.S. mail |
| | Other | | Other |

## Miscellaneous

_____

_____

_____

# The Online Journey II

## Member Rating: 1 2 3 4 5 6 7 8 9 10 / ☺ ☺ ☹

Initial thought of profile:

_____

Initial thought of correspondence:

_____

What I like most:

_____

What I like least:

_____

## Comments
### Document key information that you want to remember.
*(i.e., great conversationalist, cried on first date, great voice, member looking for long-term relationship, etc.)*

_____
_____
_____
_____
_____
_____
_____
_____
_____
_____

## Blocked Member Details

Date: _____  Blocking Method: _____

Reasons/Details:

_____
_____
_____

# The Online Journey I

## Contact Data

Screen Name: _____     Legal Name: _____

Online Dating Service: _____     Date contact initiated: _____

☐ I initiated contact     ☐ He/She initiated contact

The reason I made contact or responded to contact:

_____

## Exchange of Personal Data

Date I sent personal data: _____     Date I received personal data: _____

Address: _____     City: _____ State: _____ Zip: _____

Age: _____     Height: _____     Other: _____

Contact Numbers:     Home: _____     Mobile: _____ Other: _____

E-mail address:

## Photo Overview

Photo ☐ Yes / ☐ No

_____

_____

## Let the Journey Begin—Number of Correspondence

| ̶H̶I̶I̶ II | Sent to contact | ̶H̶I̶I̶ II | Received from contact |
|---|---|---|---|
| | E-mail messages | | E-mail messages |
| | Emoticons (winks, smiles, etc.) | | Emoticons (winks, smiles, etc.) |
| | Phone calls | | Phone calls |
| | Virtual dates initiated | | Virtual dates initiated |
| | Live dates initiated | | Live dates initiated |
| | U.S. mail | | U.S. mail |
| | Other | | Other |

## Miscellaneous

_____

_____

_____

# The Online Journey II

Initial thought of profile:
_____

Initial thought of correspondence:
_____

What I like most:
_____

What I like least:
_____

## Comments

Document key information that you want to remember.
*(i.e., great conversationalist, cried on first date, great voice, member looking for long-term relationship, etc.)*

_____
_____
_____
_____
_____
_____
_____
_____
_____
_____

## Blocked Member Details

Date: _____    Blocking Method: _____

Reasons/Details:
_____
_____
_____

# The Online Journey I

## Contact Data

Screen Name: _____     Legal Name: _____

Online Dating Service: _____     Date contact initiated: _____

☐ I initiated contact     ☐ He/She initiated contact

The reason I made contact or responded to contact:

_____

## Exchange of Personal Data

Date I sent personal data: _____     Date I received personal data: _____

Address: _____     City: _____ State: _____ Zip: _____

Age: _____     Height: _____     Other: _____

Contact Numbers:     Home: _____     Mobile: _____     Other: _____

E-mail address:

## Photo Overview

Photo ☐ Yes / ☐ No

_____

_____

## Let the Journey Begin—Number of Correspondence

| ̶I̶I̶I̶ II | Sent to contact | ̶I̶I̶I̶ II | Received from contact |
|---|---|---|---|
| | E-mail messages | | E-mail messages |
| | Emoticons (winks, smiles, etc.) | | Emoticons (winks, smiles, etc.) |
| | Phone calls | | Phone calls |
| | Virtual dates initiated | | Virtual dates initiated |
| | Live dates initiated | | Live dates initiated |
| | U.S. mail | | U.S. mail |
| | Other | | Other |

## Miscellaneous

_____

_____

_____

# The Online Journey II

**Member Rating:** 1 2 3 4 5 6 7 8 9 10 / ☺ 😐 ☹

Initial thought of profile:
_____

Initial thought of correspondence:
_____

What I like most:
_____

What I like least:
_____

## Comments
Document key information that you want to remember.
*(i.e., great conversationalist, cried on first date, great voice, member looking for long-term relationship, etc.)*

_____
_____
_____
_____
_____
_____
_____
_____
_____

## Blocked Member Details

Date: _____     Blocking Method: _____

Reasons/Details:
_____
_____
_____

# The Online Journey I

## Contact Data

Screen Name: _____  Legal Name: _____

Online Dating Service: _____  Date contact initiated: _____

☐ I initiated contact  ☐ He/She initiated contact

The reason I made contact or responded to contact:

_____

## Exchange of Personal Data

Date I sent personal data: _____  Date I received personal data: _____

Address: _____  City: _____  State: _____  Zip: _____

Age: _____  Height: _____  Other: _____

Contact Numbers:  Home: _____  Mobile: _____  Other: _____

E-mail address:

## Photo Overview

Photo ☐ Yes / ☐ No

_____
_____

## Let the Journey Begin—Number of Correspondence

| ̶H̶T̶ II | Sent to contact | ̶H̶T̶ II | Received from contact |
|---|---|---|---|
| | E-mail messages | | E-mail messages |
| | Emoticons (winks, smiles, etc.) | | Emoticons (winks, smiles, etc.) |
| | Phone calls | | Phone calls |
| | Virtual dates initiated | | Virtual dates initiated |
| | Live dates initiated | | Live dates initiated |
| | U.S. mail | | U.S. mail |
| | Other | | Other |

## Miscellaneous

_____
_____
_____

# The Online Journey II

Member Rating: 1 2 3 4 5 6 7 8 9 10 / ☺ ☺ ☹

Initial thought of profile:
_____

Initial thought of correspondence:
_____

What I like most:
_____

What I like least:
_____

## Comments
Document key information that you want to remember.
*(i.e., great conversationalist, cried on first date, great voice, member looking for long-term relationship, etc.)*

_____
_____
_____
_____
_____
_____
_____
_____
_____
_____

## Blocked Member Details

Date: _____    Blocking Method: _____

Reasons/Details:
_____
_____
_____

# The Online Journey I

## Contact Data

Screen Name: _____  Legal Name: _____

Online Dating Service: _____  Date contact initiated: _____

☐ I initiated contact    ☐ He/She initiated contact

The reason I made contact or responded to contact:

_____

## Exchange of Personal Data

Date I sent personal data: _____  Date I received personal data: _____

Address: _____  City: _____  State: _____  Zip: _____

Age: _____    Height: _____  Other: _____

Contact Numbers:    Home: _____  Mobile: _____  Other: _____

E-mail address:

## Photo Overview

Photo ☐ Yes / ☐ No

_____

_____

## Let the Journey Begin—Number of Correspondence

| ̶H̶I̶I | Sent to contact | ̶H̶I̶I | Received from contact |
|---|---|---|---|
| | E-mail messages | | E-mail messages |
| | Emoticons (winks, smiles, etc.) | | Emoticons (winks, smiles, etc.) |
| | Phone calls | | Phone calls |
| | Virtual dates initiated | | Virtual dates initiated |
| | Live dates initiated | | Live dates initiated |
| | U.S. mail | | U.S. mail |
| | Other | | Other |

## Miscellaneous

_____

_____

_____

# The Online Journey II

**Member Rating: 1 2 3 4 5 6 7 8 9 10 / ☺ 😐 ☹**

Initial thought of profile:
_____

Initial thought of correspondence:
_____

What I like most:
_____

What I like least:
_____

## Comments
Document key information that you want to remember.
*(i.e., great conversationalist, cried on first date, great voice, member looking for long-term relationship, etc.)*

_____
_____
_____
_____
_____
_____
_____
_____
_____
_____

## Blocked Member Details

Date: _____    Blocking Method: _____

Reasons/Details:
_____
_____
_____

*Have you been on a Virtual Date?*

# The Online Journey I

## Contact Data

Screen Name: _____     Legal Name: _____

Online Dating Service: _____     Date contact initiated: _____

☐ I initiated contact     ☐ He/She initiated contact

The reason I made contact or responded to contact:

_____

## Exchange of Personal Data

Date I sent personal data: _____     Date I received personal data: _____

Address: _____     City: _____ State: _____ Zip: _____

Age: _____     Height: _____     Other: _____

Contact Numbers:     Home: _____     Mobile: _____ Other: _____

E-mail address:

## Photo Overview

Photo ☐ Yes / ☐ No

_____

_____

## Let the Journey Begin—Number of Correspondence

| ~~IIII~~ II | Sent to contact | ~~IIII~~ II | Received from contact |
|---|---|---|---|
| | E-mail messages | | E-mail messages |
| | Emoticons (winks, smiles, etc.) | | Emoticons (winks, smiles, etc.) |
| | Phone calls | | Phone calls |
| | Virtual dates initiated | | Virtual dates initiated |
| | Live dates initiated | | Live dates initiated |
| | U.S. mail | | U.S. mail |
| | Other | | Other |

## Miscellaneous

_____

_____

_____

# The Online Journey II

Member Rating: 1 2 3 4 5 6 7 8 9 10 / ☺ ☺ ☹

Initial thought of profile:

_____

Initial thought of correspondence:

_____

What I like most:

_____

What I like least:

_____

## Comments

Document key information that you want to remember.
*(i.e., great conversationalist, cried on first date, great voice, member looking for long-term relationship, etc.)*

_____
_____
_____
_____
_____
_____
_____
_____
_____
_____

## Blocked Member Details

Date: _____ Blocking Method: _____

Reasons/Details:

_____
_____
_____

# The Online Journey I

## Contact Data

Screen Name: _____     Legal Name: _____

Online Dating Service: _____     Date contact initiated: _____

☐ I initiated contact     ☐ He/She initiated contact

The reason I made contact or responded to contact:

_____

## Exchange of Personal Data

Date I sent personal data: _____     Date I received personal data: _____

Address: _____     City: _____  State: _____  Zip: _____

Age: _____     Height: _____     Other: _____

Contact Numbers:     Home: _____     Mobile: _____     Other: _____

E-mail address:

### Photo Overview

Photo ☐ Yes / ☐ No

_____
_____

## Let the Journey Begin—Number of Correspondence

| ~~IIII~~ II | Sent to contact | ~~IIII~~ II | Received from contact |
|---|---|---|---|
| | E-mail messages | | E-mail messages |
| | Emoticons (winks, smiles, etc.) | | Emoticons (winks, smiles, etc.) |
| | Phone calls | | Phone calls |
| | Virtual dates initiated | | Virtual dates initiated |
| | Live dates initiated | | Live dates initiated |
| | U.S. mail | | U.S. mail |
| | Other | | Other |

### Miscellaneous

_____
_____
_____

# The Online Journey II

Initial thought of profile:
_____

Initial thought of correspondence:
_____

What I like most:
_____

What I like least:
_____

## Comments

Document key information that you want to remember.
*(i.e., great conversationalist, cried on first date, great voice, member looking for long-term relationship, etc.)*

_____
_____
_____
_____
_____
_____
_____
_____
_____

## Blocked Member Details

Date: _____    Blocking Method: _____

Reasons/Details:
_____
_____
_____

# The Online Journey I

## Contact Data

Screen Name: _____     Legal Name: _____

Online Dating Service: _____     Date contact initiated: _____

☐ I initiated contact     ☐ He/She initiated contact

The reason I made contact or responded to contact:

_____

## Exchange of Personal Data

Date I sent personal data: _____     Date I received personal data: _____

Address: _____     City: _____  State: _____  Zip: _____

Age: _____     Height: _____     Other: _____

Contact Numbers:     Home: _____     Mobile: _____     Other: _____

E-mail address:

## Photo Overview

Photo ☐ Yes / ☐ No

_____
_____

## Let the Journey Begin—Number of Correspondence

| ̶L̶H̶T̶ II | Sent to contact | ̶L̶H̶T̶ II | Received from contact |
|---|---|---|---|
| | E-mail messages | | E-mail messages |
| | Emoticons (winks, smiles, etc.) | | Emoticons (winks, smiles, etc.) |
| | Phone calls | | Phone calls |
| | Virtual dates initiated | | Virtual dates initiated |
| | Live dates initiated | | Live dates initiated |
| | U.S. mail | | U.S. mail |
| | Other | | Other |

## Miscellaneous

_____
_____
_____

# The Online Journey II

Initial thought of profile:

_____

Initial thought of correspondence:

_____

What I like most:

_____

What I like least:

_____

## Comments

Document key information that you want to remember.
*(i.e., great conversationalist, cried on first date, great voice, member looking for long-term relationship, etc.)*

_____
_____
_____
_____
_____
_____
_____
_____
_____
_____

## Blocked Member Details

Date: _____     Blocking Method: _____

Reasons/Details:

_____
_____
_____

# The Online Journey I

## Contact Data

Screen Name: _____ Legal Name: _____

Online Dating Service: _____ Date contact initiated: _____

☐ I initiated contact    ☐ He/She initiated contact

The reason I made contact or responded to contact:

_____

## Exchange of Personal Data

Date I sent personal data: _____ Date I received personal data: _____

Address: _____ City: _____ State: _____ Zip: _____

Age: _____ Height: _____ Other: _____

Contact Numbers:  Home: _____ Mobile: _____ Other: _____

E-mail address:

## Photo Overview

Photo ☐ Yes / ☐ No

_____

_____

## Let the Journey Begin—Number of Correspondence

| ~~IIII~~ II | Sent to contact | ~~IIII~~ II | Received from contact |
|---|---|---|---|
| | E-mail messages | | E-mail messages |
| | Emoticons (winks, smiles, etc.) | | Emoticons (winks, smiles, etc.) |
| | Phone calls | | Phone calls |
| | Virtual dates initiated | | Virtual dates initiated |
| | Live dates initiated | | Live dates initiated |
| | U.S. mail | | U.S. mail |
| | Other | | Other |

## Miscellaneous

_____

_____

_____

# The Online Journey II

Initial thought of profile:
_____

Initial thought of correspondence:
_____

What I like most:
_____

What I like least:
_____

## Comments

Document key information that you want to remember.
*(i.e., great conversationalist, cried on first date, great voice, member looking for long-term relationship, etc.)*

_____
_____
_____
_____
_____
_____
_____
_____
_____

## Blocked Member Details

Date: _____    Blocking Method: _____

Reasons/Details:
_____
_____
_____

# The Online Journey I

## Contact Data

Screen Name: _____          Legal Name: _____

Online Dating Service: _____          Date contact initiated: _____

☐ I initiated contact      ☐ He/She initiated contact

The reason I made contact or responded to contact:

_____

## Exchange of Personal Data

Date I sent personal data: _____          Date I received personal data: _____

Address: _____          City: _____  State: _____  Zip: _____

Age: _____          Height: _____          Other: _____

Contact Numbers:     Home: _____          Mobile: _____     Other: _____

E-mail address:

## Photo Overview

Photo ☐ Yes / ☐ No

_____

_____

## Let the Journey Begin—Number of Correspondence

| ̶H̶I̶I̶I̶ II | Sent to contact | ̶H̶I̶I̶I̶ II | Received from contact |
|---|---|---|---|
| | E-mail messages | | E-mail messages |
| | Emoticons (winks, smiles, etc.) | | Emoticons (winks, smiles, etc.) |
| | Phone calls | | Phone calls |
| | Virtual dates initiated | | Virtual dates initiated |
| | Live dates initiated | | Live dates initiated |
| | U.S. mail | | U.S. mail |
| | Other | | Other |

## Miscellaneous

_____

_____

_____

# The Online Journey II

Member Rating: 1 2 3 4 5 6 7 8 9 10 / ☺ ☺ ☹

Initial thought of profile:

_____

Initial thought of correspondence:

_____

What I like most:

_____

What I like least:

_____

## Comments

Document key information that you want to remember.
*(i.e., great conversationalist, cried on first date, great voice, member looking for long-term relationship, etc.)*

_____
_____
_____
_____
_____
_____
_____
_____
_____

## Blocked Member Details

Date: _____ Blocking Method: _____

Reasons/Details:

_____
_____
_____

*Never, ever settle.*

# The Online Journey I

## Contact Data

Screen Name: _____     Legal Name: _____

Online Dating Service: _____     Date contact initiated: _____

☐ I initiated contact     ☐ He/She initiated contact

The reason I made contact or responded to contact:

_____

## Exchange of Personal Data

Date I sent personal data: _____     Date I received personal data: _____

Address: _____     City: _____  State: _____  Zip: _____

Age: _____  Height: _____     Other: _____

Contact Numbers:  Home: _____     Mobile: _____  Other: _____

E-mail address:

## Photo Overview

Photo ☐ Yes / ☐ No

_____
_____

## Let the Journey Begin—Number of Correspondence

| ⳤ̷ ‖ | Sent to contact | ⳤ̷ ‖ | Received from contact |
|---|---|---|---|
|  | E-mail messages |  | E-mail messages |
|  | Emoticons (winks, smiles, etc.) |  | Emoticons (winks, smiles, etc.) |
|  | Phone calls |  | Phone calls |
|  | Virtual dates initiated |  | Virtual dates initiated |
|  | Live dates initiated |  | Live dates initiated |
|  | U.S. mail |  | U.S. mail |
|  | Other |  | Other |

## Miscellaneous

_____
_____
_____

# The Online Journey II

Initial thought of profile:

_____

Initial thought of correspondence:

_____

What I like most:

_____

What I like least:

_____

## Comments

### Document key information that you want to remember.
*(i.e., great conversationalist, cried on first date, great voice, member looking for long-term relationship, etc.)*

_____
_____
_____
_____
_____
_____
_____
_____
_____
_____

## Blocked Member Details

Date: _____  Blocking Method: _____

Reasons/Details:

_____
_____
_____

# The Online Journey I

Screen Name: _____     Legal Name: _____

Online Dating Service: _____     Date contact initiated: _____

☐ I initiated contact     ☐ He/She initiated contact

The reason I made contact or responded to contact:

_____

_____

## Exchange of Personal Data

Date I sent personal data: _____     Date I received personal data: _____

Address: _____     City: _____ State: _____ Zip: _____

Age: _____     Height: _____     Other: _____

Contact Numbers:     Home: _____     Mobile: _____ Other: _____

E-mail address:

### Photo Overview

Photo ☐ Yes / ☐ No

_____

_____

## Let the Journey Begin—Number of Correspondence

| J̶H̶T̶ II | Sent to contact | J̶H̶T̶ II | Received from contact |
|---|---|---|---|
| | E-mail messages | | E-mail messages |
| | Emoticons (winks, smiles, etc.) | | Emoticons (winks, smiles, etc.) |
| | Phone calls | | Phone calls |
| | Virtual dates initiated | | Virtual dates initiated |
| | Live dates initiated | | Live dates initiated |
| | U.S. mail | | U.S. mail |
| | Other | | Other |

## Miscellaneous

_____

_____

_____

## The Online Journey II

Member Rating: 1 2 3 4 5 6 7 8 9 10 / ☺ ☺ ☹

Initial thought of profile:
_____

Initial thought of correspondence:
_____

What I like most:
_____

What I like least:
_____

### Comments

Document key information that you want to remember.
*(i.e., great conversationalist, cried on first date, great voice, member looking for long-term relationship, etc.)*

_____
_____
_____
_____
_____
_____
_____
_____
_____

### Blocked Member Details

Date: _____    Blocking Method: _____

Reasons/Details:
_____
_____
_____

# The Online Journey I

## Contact Data

Screen Name: _____    Legal Name: _____

Online Dating Service: _____    Date contact initiated: _____

☐ I initiated contact    ☐ He/She initiated contact

The reason I made contact or responded to contact:

_____

## Exchange of Personal Data

Date I sent personal data: _____    Date I received personal data: _____

Address: _____    City: _____   State: _____   Zip: _____

Age: _____    Height: _____    Other: _____

Contact Numbers:   Home: _____    Mobile: _____    Other: _____

E-mail address:

## Photo Overview

Photo ☐ Yes / ☐ No

_____

_____

## Let the Journey Begin—Number of Correspondence

| ⅦⅠ II | Sent to contact | ⅦⅠ II | Received from contact |
|---|---|---|---|
| | E-mail messages | | E-mail messages |
| | Emoticons (winks, smiles, etc.) | | Emoticons (winks, smiles, etc.) |
| | Phone calls | | Phone calls |
| | Virtual dates initiated | | Virtual dates initiated |
| | Live dates initiated | | Live dates initiated |
| | U.S. mail | | U.S. mail |
| | Other | | Other |

## Miscellaneous

_____

_____

_____

# The Online Journey II

Initial thought of profile:
_____

Initial thought of correspondence:
_____

What I like most:
_____

What I like least:
_____

## Comments
Document key information that you want to remember.
*(i.e., great conversationalist, cried on first date, great voice, member looking for long-term relationship, etc.)*

_____
_____
_____
_____
_____
_____
_____
_____
_____

## Blocked Member Details

Date: _____    Blocking Method: _____

Reasons/Details:
_____
_____
_____

# The Online Journey I

## Contact Data

Screen Name: _____   Legal Name: _____

Online Dating Service: _____   Date contact initiated: _____

☐ I initiated contact   ☐ He/She initiated contact

The reason I made contact or responded to contact:

_____

## Exchange of Personal Data

Date I sent personal data: _____   Date I received personal data: _____

Address: _____   City: _____ State: _____ Zip: _____

Age: _____   Height: _____   Other: _____

Contact Numbers:   Home: _____   Mobile: _____   Other: _____

E-mail address:

## Photo Overview

Photo ☐ Yes / ☐ No

_____

_____

## Let the Journey Begin—Number of Correspondence

| ~~IIII~~ II | Sent to contact | ~~IIII~~ II | Received from contact |
|---|---|---|---|
| | E-mail messages | | E-mail messages |
| | Emoticons (winks, smiles, etc.) | | Emoticons (winks, smiles, etc.) |
| | Phone calls | | Phone calls |
| | Virtual dates initiated | | Virtual dates initiated |
| | Live dates initiated | | Live dates initiated |
| | U.S. mail | | U.S. mail |
| | Other | | Other |

## Miscellaneous

_____

_____

_____

# The Online Journey II

Initial thought of profile:

_____

Initial thought of correspondence:

_____

What I like most:

_____

What I like least:

_____

## Comments

Document key information that you want to remember.
*(i.e., great conversationalist, cried on first date, great voice, member looking for long-term relationship, etc.)*

_____
_____
_____
_____
_____
_____
_____
_____
_____

## Blocked Member Details

Date: _____     Blocking Method: _____

Reasons/Details:

_____
_____
_____

What are your overall experiences with online dating?

# Online Dating Experiences

_____

_____

_____

_____

_____

_____

_____

_____

_____

_____

_____

# The Online Journey I

## Contact Data

Screen Name: _____     Legal Name: _____

Online Dating Service: _____     Date contact initiated: _____

☐ I initiated contact     ☐ He/She initiated contact

The reason I made contact or responded to contact:

_____

## Exchange of Personal Data

Date I sent personal data: _____     Date I received personal data: _____

Address: _____     City: _____ State: _____ Zip: _____

Age: _____     Height: _____     Other: _____

Contact Numbers:     Home: _____     Mobile: _____     Other: _____

E-mail address:

## Photo Overview

Photo ☐ Yes / ☐ No

_____

_____

## Let the Journey Begin—Number of Correspondence

| ~~IIII~~ II | Sent to contact | ~~IIII~~ II | Received from contact |
|---|---|---|---|
| | E-mail messages | | E-mail messages |
| | Emoticons (winks, smiles, etc.) | | Emoticons (winks, smiles, etc.) |
| | Phone calls | | Phone calls |
| | Virtual dates initiated | | Virtual dates initiated |
| | Live dates initiated | | Live dates initiated |
| | U.S. mail | | U.S. mail |
| | Other | | Other |

## Miscellaneous

_____

_____

_____

# The Online Journey II

Initial thought of profile:
_____

Initial thought of correspondence:
_____

What I like most:
_____

What I like least:
_____

## Comments

Document key information that you want to remember.
*(i.e., great conversationalist, cried on first date, great voice, member looking for long-term relationship, etc.)*

_____
_____
_____
_____
_____
_____
_____
_____
_____
_____

## Blocked Member Details

Date: _____   Blocking Method: _____

Reasons/Details:
_____
_____
_____

*What an exciting time to be dating!*

# The Online Journey I

## Contact Data

Screen Name: _____     Legal Name: _____

Online Dating Service: _____     Date contact initiated: _____

☐ I initiated contact     ☐ He/She initiated contact

The reason I made contact or responded to contact:

_____

## Exchange of Personal Data

Date I sent personal data: _____     Date I received personal data: _____

Address: _____     City: _____ State: _____ Zip: _____

Age: _____     Height: _____     Other: _____

Contact Numbers: Home: _____     Mobile: _____ Other: _____

E-mail address:

## Photo Overview

Photo ☐ Yes / ☐ No

_____
_____

## Let the Journey Begin—Number of Correspondence

| ⵏⵏⵏ II | Sent to contact | ⵏⵏⵏ II | Received from contact |
|---|---|---|---|
| | E-mail messages | | E-mail messages |
| | Emoticons (winks, smiles, etc.) | | Emoticons (winks, smiles, etc.) |
| | Phone calls | | Phone calls |
| | Virtual dates initiated | | Virtual dates initiated |
| | Live dates initiated | | Live dates initiated |
| | U.S. mail | | U.S. mail |
| | Other | | Other |

## Miscellaneous

_____
_____
_____

# The Online Journey II

Initial thought of profile:
_____

Initial thought of correspondence:
_____

What I like most:
_____

What I like least:
_____

## Comments

Document key information that you want to remember.
*(i.e., great conversationalist, cried on first date, great voice, member looking for long-term relationship, etc.)*

_____
_____
_____
_____
_____
_____
_____
_____
_____
_____

## Blocked Member Details

Date: _____  Blocking Method: _____

Reasons/Details:
_____
_____
_____

# The Online Journey I

## Contact Data

Screen Name: ______________________ Legal Name: ______________________

Online Dating Service: ______________ Date contact initiated: ________________

☐ I initiated contact ☐ He/She initiated contact

The reason I made contact or responded to contact:

_______________________________________________________________

## Exchange of Personal Data

Date I sent personal data: _____________ Date I received personal data: ________________

Address: ___________________________ City: _________ State: ______ Zip: ______

Age: _________ Height: _________ Other: ______________________________

Contact Numbers: Home: _________ Mobile: ______________ Other: ___________

E-mail address:

## Photo Overview

Photo ☐ Yes / ☐ No

_______________________________________________________________

_______________________________________________________________

## Let the Journey Begin—Number of Correspondence

| ~~\|\|\|\|~~ \|\| | Sent to contact | ~~\|\|\|\|~~ \|\| | Received from contact |
|---|---|---|---|
| | E-mail messages | | E-mail messages |
| | Emoticons (winks, smiles, etc.) | | Emoticons (winks, smiles, etc.) |
| | Phone calls | | Phone calls |
| | Virtual dates initiated | | Virtual dates initiated |
| | Live dates initiated | | Live dates initiated |
| | U.S. mail | | U.S. mail |
| | Other | | Other |

## Miscellaneous

_______________________________________________________________

_______________________________________________________________

_______________________________________________________________

# The Online Journey II

Initial thought of profile:

_____

Initial thought of correspondence:

_____

What I like most:

_____

What I like least:

_____

## Comments

Document key information that you want to remember.
*(i.e., great conversationalist, cried on first date, great voice, member looking for long-term relationship, etc.)*

_____
_____
_____
_____
_____
_____
_____
_____
_____
_____

## Blocked Member Details

Date: _____  Blocking Method: _____

Reasons/Details:

_____
_____
_____

# The Online Journey I

## Contact Data

Screen Name: _____    Legal Name: _____

Online Dating Service: _____    Date contact initiated: _____

☐ I initiated contact    ☐ He/She initiated contact

The reason I made contact or responded to contact:

_____

## Exchange of Personal Data

Date I sent personal data: _____    Date I received personal data: _____

Address: _____    City: _____  State: _____  Zip: _____

Age: _____    Height: _____    Other: _____

Contact Numbers:    Home: _____    Mobile: _____    Other: _____

E-mail address:

## Photo Overview

Photo ☐ Yes / ☐ No

_____

_____

## Let the Journey Begin—Number of Correspondence

| ~~||||~~ || | Sent to contact | ~~||||~~ || | Received from contact |
|---|---|---|---|
| | E-mail messages | | E-mail messages |
| | Emoticons (winks, smiles, etc.) | | Emoticons (winks, smiles, etc.) |
| | Phone calls | | Phone calls |
| | Virtual dates initiated | | Virtual dates initiated |
| | Live dates initiated | | Live dates initiated |
| | U.S. mail | | U.S. mail |
| | Other | | Other |

## Miscellaneous

_____

_____

_____

# The Online Journey II

Initial thought of profile:
_____

Initial thought of correspondence:
_____

What I like most:
_____

What I like least:
_____

## Comments

Document key information that you want to remember.
*(i.e., great conversationalist, cried on first date, great voice, member looking for long-term relationship, etc.)*

_____
_____
_____
_____
_____
_____
_____
_____
_____

## Blocked Member Details

Date: _____     Blocking Method: _____

Reasons/Details:
_____
_____
_____

237

# The Online Journey I

## Contact Data

Screen Name: _____     Legal Name: _____

Online Dating Service: _____     Date contact initiated: _____

☐ I initiated contact     ☐ He/She initiated contact

The reason I made contact or responded to contact:

_____

## Exchange of Personal Data

Date I sent personal data: _____     Date I received personal data: _____

Address: _____     City: _____   State: _____   Zip: _____

Age: _____     Height: _____     Other: _____

Contact Numbers:     Home: _____     Mobile: _____     Other: _____

E-mail address:

## Photo Overview

Photo ☐ Yes / ☐ No

_____

_____

## Let the Journey Begin—Number of Correspondence

| ||||̷ || | Sent to contact | ||||̷ || | Received from contact |
|---|---|---|---|
| | E-mail messages | | E-mail messages |
| | Emoticons (winks, smiles, etc.) | | Emoticons (winks, smiles, etc.) |
| | Phone calls | | Phone calls |
| | Virtual dates initiated | | Virtual dates initiated |
| | Live dates initiated | | Live dates initiated |
| | U.S. mail | | U.S. mail |
| | Other | | Other |

## Miscellaneous

_____

_____

_____

# The Online Journey II

Initial thought of profile:

_____

Initial thought of correspondence:

_____

What I like most:

_____

What I like least:

_____

## Comments
Document key information that you want to remember.
*(i.e., great conversationalist, cried on first date, great voice, member looking for long-term relationship, etc.)*

_____
_____
_____
_____
_____
_____
_____
_____
_____
_____

## Blocked Member Details

Date: _____     Blocking Method: _____

Reasons/Details:

_____
_____
_____

# The Online Journey I

## Contact Data

Screen Name: _____      Legal Name: _____

Online Dating Service: _____      Date contact initiated: _____

☐ I initiated contact      ☐ He/She initiated contact

The reason I made contact or responded to contact:

_____

## Exchange of Personal Data

Date I sent personal data: _____      Date I received personal data: _____

Address: _____      City: _____      State: _____      Zip: _____

Age: _____      Height: _____      Other: _____

Contact Numbers:      Home: _____      Mobile: _____      Other: _____

E-mail address:

## Photo Overview

Photo ☐ Yes / ☐ No

_____

_____

## Let the Journey Begin—Number of Correspondence

| ~~JHT~~ II | Sent to contact | ~~JHT~~ II | Received from contact |
|---|---|---|---|
|  | E-mail messages |  | E-mail messages |
|  | Emoticons (winks, smiles, etc.) |  | Emoticons (winks, smiles, etc.) |
|  | Phone calls |  | Phone calls |
|  | Virtual dates initiated |  | Virtual dates initiated |
|  | Live dates initiated |  | Live dates initiated |
|  | U.S. mail |  | U.S. mail |
|  | Other |  | Other |

## Miscellaneous

_____

_____

_____

# The Online Journey II

Member Rating: 1 2 3 4 5 6 7 8 9 10 / ☺ ☺ ☹

Initial thought of profile:
_____

Initial thought of correspondence:
_____

What I like most:
_____

What I like least:
_____

## Comments

### Document key information that you want to remember.
*(i.e., great conversationalist, cried on first date, great voice, member looking for long-term relationship, etc.)*

_____
_____
_____
_____
_____
_____
_____
_____
_____
_____

## Blocked Member Details

Date: _____    Blocking Method: _____

Reasons/Details:
_____
_____
_____

*Celebrate life! Live it to the fullest.*

# The Online Journey I

## Contact Data

Screen Name: _____     Legal Name: _____

Online Dating Service: _____     Date contact initiated: _____

☐ I initiated contact     ☐ He/She initiated contact

The reason I made contact or responded to contact:

_____

## Exchange of Personal Data

Date I sent personal data: _____     Date I received personal data: _____

Address: _____     City: _____  State: _____  Zip: _____

Age: _____     Height: _____     Other: _____

Contact Numbers:     Home: _____     Mobile: _____  Other: _____

E-mail address:

## Photo Overview

Photo ☐ Yes / ☐ No

_____

_____

## Let the Journey Begin—Number of Correspondence

| ~~IIII~~ II | Sent to contact | ~~IIII~~ II | Received from contact |
|---|---|---|---|
| | E-mail messages | | E-mail messages |
| | Emoticons (winks, smiles, etc.) | | Emoticons (winks, smiles, etc.) |
| | Phone calls | | Phone calls |
| | Virtual dates initiated | | Virtual dates initiated |
| | Live dates initiated | | Live dates initiated |
| | U.S. mail | | U.S. mail |
| | Other | | Other |

## Miscellaneous

_____

_____

_____

# The Online Journey II

Initial thought of profile:

_____

Initial thought of correspondence:

_____

What I like most:

_____

What I like least:

_____

## Comments
Document key information that you want to remember.
*(i.e., great conversationalist, cried on first date, great voice, member looking for long-term relationship, etc.)*

_____
_____
_____
_____
_____
_____
_____
_____
_____

## Blocked Member Details

Date: _____    Blocking Method: _____

Reasons/Details:

_____
_____
_____

# The Online Journey I

## Contact Data

Screen Name: _____     Legal Name: _____

Online Dating Service: _____     Date contact initiated: _____

☐ I initiated contact     ☐ He/She initiated contact

The reason I made contact or responded to contact:

_____

## Exchange of Personal Data

Date I sent personal data: _____     Date I received personal data: _____

Address: _____     City: _____  State: _____  Zip: _____

Age: _____     Height: _____     Other: _____

Contact Numbers:     Home: _____     Mobile: _____     Other: _____

E-mail address:

## Photo Overview

Photo ☐ Yes / ☐ No

_____

_____

## Let the Journey Begin—Number of Correspondence

| ~~IIII~~ II | Sent to contact | ~~IIII~~ II | Received from contact |
|---|---|---|---|
| | E-mail messages | | E-mail messages |
| | Emoticons (winks, smiles, etc.) | | Emoticons (winks, smiles, etc.) |
| | Phone calls | | Phone calls |
| | Virtual dates initiated | | Virtual dates initiated |
| | Live dates initiated | | Live dates initiated |
| | U.S. mail | | U.S. mail |
| | Other | | Other |

## Miscellaneous

_____

_____

_____

# The Online Journey II

Initial thought of profile:
_____

Initial thought of correspondence:
_____

What I like most:
_____

What I like least:
_____

## Comments

Document key information that you want to remember.
*(i.e., great conversationalist, cried on first date, great voice, member looking for long-term relationship, etc.)*

_____
_____
_____
_____
_____
_____
_____
_____
_____

## Blocked Member Details

Date: _____   Blocking Method: _____

Reasons/Details:
_____
_____
_____

## The Online Journey I

### Contact Data

Screen Name: _____     Legal Name: _____

Online Dating Service: _____     Date contact initiated: _____

☐ I initiated contact     ☐ He/She initiated contact

The reason I made contact or responded to contact:

_____

### Exchange of Personal Data

Date I sent personal data: _____     Date I received personal data: _____

Address: _____     City: _____ State: _____ Zip: _____

Age: _____    Height: _____    Other: _____

Contact Numbers:   Home: _____    Mobile: _____ Other: _____

E-mail address:

### Photo Overview

Photo ☐ Yes / ☐ No

_____

_____

### Let the Journey Begin—Number of Correspondence

| ⳤ̶||  | Sent to contact | ⳤ̶|| | Received from contact |
|------|-----------------|------|-----------------------|
|      | E-mail messages |      | E-mail messages |
|      | Emoticons (winks, smiles, etc.) | | Emoticons (winks, smiles, etc.) |
|      | Phone calls     |      | Phone calls |
|      | Virtual dates initiated | | Virtual dates initiated |
|      | Live dates initiated | | Live dates initiated |
|      | U.S. mail       |      | U.S. mail |
|      | Other           |      | Other |

### Miscellaneous

_____

_____

_____

# The Online Journey II

Member Rating: 1 2 3 4 5 6 7 8 9 10 / ☺ ☺ ☹

Initial thought of profile:
_____

Initial thought of correspondence:
_____

What I like most:
_____

What I like least:
_____

## Comments

Document key information that you want to remember.
*(i.e., great conversationalist, cried on first date, great voice, member looking for long-term relationship, etc.)*

_____
_____
_____
_____
_____
_____
_____
_____
_____
_____

## Blocked Member Details

Date: _____ Blocking Method: _____

Reasons/Details:
_____
_____
_____

# The Online Journey I

## Contact Data

Screen Name: _____     Legal Name: _____

Online Dating Service: _____     Date contact initiated: _____

☐ I initiated contact     ☐ He/She initiated contact

The reason I made contact or responded to contact:

_____

## Exchange of Personal Data

Date I sent personal data: _____     Date I received personal data: _____

Address: _____     City: _____     State: _____     Zip: _____

Age: _____     Height: _____     Other: _____

Contact Numbers:     Home: _____     Mobile: _____     Other: _____

E-mail address:

## Photo Overview

Photo ☐ Yes / ☐ No

_____

_____

## Let the Journey Begin—Number of Correspondence

| ⦀|| | Sent to contact | ⦀|| | Received from contact |
|---|---|---|---|
| | E-mail messages | | E-mail messages |
| | Emoticons (winks, smiles, etc.) | | Emoticons (winks, smiles, etc.) |
| | Phone calls | | Phone calls |
| | Virtual dates initiated | | Virtual dates initiated |
| | Live dates initiated | | Live dates initiated |
| | U.S. mail | | U.S. mail |
| | Other | | Other |

## Miscellaneous

_____

_____

_____

# The Online Journey II

Initial thought of profile:

_____

Initial thought of correspondence:

_____

What I like most:

_____

What I like least:

_____

## Comments

Document key information that you want to remember.
*(i.e., great conversationalist, cried on first date, great voice, member looking for long-term relationship, etc.)*

_____
_____
_____
_____
_____
_____
_____
_____
_____

## Blocked Member Details

Date: _____    Blocking Method: _____

Reasons/Details:

_____
_____
_____

# The Online Journey I

## Contact Data

Screen Name: _____     Legal Name: _____

Online Dating Service: _____     Date contact initiated: _____

☐ I initiated contact     ☐ He/She initiated contact

The reason I made contact or responded to contact:

_____

## Exchange of Personal Data

Date I sent personal data: _____     Date I received personal data: _____

Address: _____     City: _____ State: _____ Zip: _____

Age: _____     Height: _____     Other: _____

Contact Numbers:     Home: _____     Mobile: _____ Other: _____

E-mail address:

### Photo Overview

Photo ☐ Yes / ☐ No

_____

_____

## Let the Journey Begin—Number of Correspondence

| ЦH̶ II | Sent to contact | ЦH̶ II | Received from contact |
|---|---|---|---|
| | E-mail messages | | E-mail messages |
| | Emoticons (winks, smiles, etc.) | | Emoticons (winks, smiles, etc.) |
| | Phone calls | | Phone calls |
| | Virtual dates initiated | | Virtual dates initiated |
| | Live dates initiated | | Live dates initiated |
| | U.S. mail | | U.S. mail |
| | Other | | Other |

## Miscellaneous

_____

_____

_____

# The Online Journey II

Member Rating: 1 2 3 4 5 6 7 8 9 10 / ☺ 😐 ☹

Initial thought of profile:
_____

Initial thought of correspondence:
_____

What I like most:
_____

What I like least:
_____

## Comments

Document key information that you want to remember.
*(i.e., great conversationalist, cried on first date, great voice, member looking for long-term relationship, etc.)*

_____
_____
_____
_____
_____
_____
_____
_____
_____
_____
_____

## Blocked Member Details

Date: _____  Blocking Method: _____

Reasons/Details:
_____
_____
_____

*Live your dream. Find your soul mate.*

# The Online Journey I

## Contact Data

Screen Name: _____     Legal Name: _____

Online Dating Service: _____     Date contact initiated: _____

☐ I initiated contact     ☐ He/She initiated contact

The reason I made contact or responded to contact:

_____

## Exchange of Personal Data

Date I sent personal data: _____    Date I received personal data: _____

Address: _____    City: _____ State: _____ Zip: _____

Age: _____    Height: _____    Other: _____

Contact Numbers:   Home: _____    Mobile: _____   Other: _____

E-mail address:

## Photo Overview

Photo ☐ Yes / ☐ No

_____

_____

## Let the Journey Begin—Number of Correspondence

| ⳾⳾⳾ II | Sent to contact | ⳾⳾⳾ II | Received from contact |
|---|---|---|---|
| | E-mail messages | | E-mail messages |
| | Emoticons (winks, smiles, etc.) | | Emoticons (winks, smiles, etc.) |
| | Phone calls | | Phone calls |
| | Virtual dates initiated | | Virtual dates initiated |
| | Live dates initiated | | Live dates initiated |
| | U.S. mail | | U.S. mail |
| | Other | | Other |

## Miscellaneous

_____

_____

_____

# The Online Journey II

Member Rating: 1 2 3 4 5 6 7 8 9 10 / ☺ ☻ ☹

Initial thought of profile:
_____

Initial thought of correspondence:
_____

What I like most:
_____

What I like least:
_____

## Comments

Document key information that you want to remember.
*(i.e., great conversationalist, cried on first date, great voice, member looking for long-term relationship, etc.)*

_____
_____
_____
_____
_____
_____
_____
_____
_____

## Blocked Member Details

Date: _____    Blocking Method: _____

Reasons/Details:
_____
_____
_____

## The Online Journey I

### Contact Data

Screen Name: _____     Legal Name: _____

Online Dating Service: _____     Date contact initiated: _____

☐ I initiated contact     ☐ He/She initiated contact

The reason I made contact or responded to contact:

_____

### Exchange of Personal Data

Date I sent personal data: _____     Date I received personal data: _____

Address: _____     City: _____     State: _____     Zip: _____

Age: _____     Height: _____     Other: _____

Contact Numbers:     Home: _____     Mobile: _____     Other: _____

E-mail address:

### Photo Overview

Photo ☐ Yes / ☐ No

_____
_____

### Let the Journey Begin—Number of Correspondence

| ̶L̶H̶T̶ ll | Sent to contact | ̶L̶H̶T̶ ll | Received from contact |
|---|---|---|---|
| | E-mail messages | | E-mail messages |
| | Emoticons (winks, smiles, etc.) | | Emoticons (winks, smiles, etc.) |
| | Phone calls | | Phone calls |
| | Virtual dates initiated | | Virtual dates initiated |
| | Live dates initiated | | Live dates initiated |
| | U.S. mail | | U.S. mail |
| | Other | | Other |

### Miscellaneous

_____
_____
_____

# The Online Journey II

Initial thought of profile:

_____

Initial thought of correspondence:

_____

What I like most:

_____

What I like least:

_____

## Comments

Document key information that you want to remember.
*(i.e., great conversationalist, cried on first date, great voice, member looking for long-term relationship, etc.)*

_____
_____
_____
_____
_____
_____
_____
_____
_____

## Blocked Member Details

Date: _____     Blocking Method: _____

Reasons/Details:

_____
_____
_____

# The Online Journey I

## Contact Data

Screen Name: _____ Legal Name: _____

Online Dating Service: _____ Date contact initiated: _____

☐ I initiated contact    ☐ He/She initiated contact

The reason I made contact or responded to contact:

_____

## Exchange of Personal Data

Date I sent personal data: _____ Date I received personal data: _____
Address: _____ City: _____ State: _____ Zip: _____
Age: _____ Height: _____ Other: _____
Contact Numbers:   Home: _____ Mobile: _____ Other: _____
E-mail address:

## Photo Overview

Photo ☐ Yes / ☐ No

_____
_____

## Let the Journey Begin—Number of Correspondence

| ~~IIII~~ II | Sent to contact | ~~IIII~~ II | Received from contact |
|---|---|---|---|
| | E-mail messages | | E-mail messages |
| | Emoticons (winks, smiles, etc.) | | Emoticons (winks, smiles, etc.) |
| | Phone calls | | Phone calls |
| | Virtual dates initiated | | Virtual dates initiated |
| | Live dates initiated | | Live dates initiated |
| | U.S. mail | | U.S. mail |
| | Other | | Other |

## Miscellaneous

_____
_____
_____

# The Online Journey II

Member Rating: 1 2 3 4 5 6 7 8 9 10 / ☺ ☺ ☹

Initial thought of profile:
_____

Initial thought of correspondence:
_____

What I like most:
_____

What I like least:
_____

## Comments
Document key information that you want to remember.
*(i.e., great conversationalist, cried on first date, great voice, member looking for long-term relationship, etc.)*

_____
_____
_____
_____
_____
_____
_____
_____
_____

## Blocked Member Details
Date: _____    Blocking Method: _____

Reasons/Details:
_____
_____
_____

# The Online Journey I

## Contact Data

Screen Name: _____     Legal Name: _____

Online Dating Service: _____     Date contact initiated: _____

☐ I initiated contact     ☐ He/She initiated contact

The reason I made contact or responded to contact:

_____

## Exchange of Personal Data

Date I sent personal data: _____     Date I received personal data: _____

Address: _____     City: _____  State: _____  Zip: _____

Age: _____     Height: _____     Other: _____

Contact Numbers:     Home: _____     Mobile: _____     Other: _____

E-mail address:

## Photo Overview

Photo ☐ Yes / ☐ No

_____
_____

## Let the Journey Begin—Number of Correspondence

| ~~|||~~ || | Sent to contact | ~~|||~~ || | Received from contact |
|---|---|---|---|
| | E-mail messages | | E-mail messages |
| | Emoticons (winks, smiles, etc.) | | Emoticons (winks, smiles, etc.) |
| | Phone calls | | Phone calls |
| | Virtual dates initiated | | Virtual dates initiated |
| | Live dates initiated | | Live dates initiated |
| | U.S. mail | | U.S. mail |
| | Other | | Other |

## Miscellaneous

_____
_____
_____

# The Online Journey II

Member Rating: 1 2 3 4 5 6 7 8 9 10 / ☺ ☺ ☹

Initial thought of profile:
_____

Initial thought of correspondence:
_____

What I like most:
_____

What I like least:
_____

## Comments
Document key information that you want to remember.
*(i.e., great conversationalist, cried on first date, great voice, member looking for long-term relationship, etc.)*
_____
_____
_____
_____
_____
_____
_____
_____
_____

## Blocked Member Details
Date: _____ Blocking Method: _____
Reasons/Details:
_____
_____
_____

# The Online Journey I

## Contact Data

Screen Name: _____     Legal Name: _____

Online Dating Service: _____     Date contact initiated: _____

☐ I initiated contact     ☐ He/She initiated contact

The reason I made contact or responded to contact:

_____

## Exchange of Personal Data

Date I sent personal data: _____     Date I received personal data: _____

Address: _____     City: _____     State: _____     Zip: _____

Age: _____     Height: _____     Other: _____

Contact Numbers:     Home: _____     Mobile: _____     Other: _____

E-mail address:

## Photo Overview

Photo ☐ Yes / ☐ No

_____

_____

## Let the Journey Begin—Number of Correspondence

| ⊬ʜ̶ ǁ | Sent to contact | ⊬ʜ̶ ǁ | Received from contact |
|---|---|---|---|
| | E-mail messages | | E-mail messages |
| | Emoticons (winks, smiles, etc.) | | Emoticons (winks, smiles, etc.) |
| | Phone calls | | Phone calls |
| | Virtual dates initiated | | Virtual dates initiated |
| | Live dates initiated | | Live dates initiated |
| | U.S. mail | | U.S. mail |
| | Other | | Other |

## Miscellaneous

_____

_____

_____

# The Online Journey II

## Member Rating: 1 2 3 4 5 6 7 8 9 10 / ☺ ☻ ☹

Initial thought of profile:
_____

Initial thought of correspondence:
_____

What I like most:
_____

What I like least:
_____

## Comments

Document key information that you want to remember.
*(i.e., great conversationalist, cried on first date, great voice, member looking for long-term relationship, etc.)*

_____
_____
_____
_____
_____
_____
_____
_____
_____

## Blocked Member Details

Date: _____    Blocking Method: _____

Reasons/Details:
_____
_____
_____

*You never have fun with something you haven't experienced; try Virtual Dating.*

# The Online Journey I

## Contact Data

Screen Name: _____    Legal Name: _____

Online Dating Service: _____    Date contact initiated: _____

☐ I initiated contact     ☐ He/She initiated contact

The reason I made contact or responded to contact:

_____

## Exchange of Personal Data

Date I sent personal data: _____    Date I received personal data: _____

Address: _____    City: _____    State: _____    Zip: _____

Age: _____    Height: _____    Other: _____

Contact Numbers:    Home: _____    Mobile: _____    Other: _____

E-mail address:

### Photo Overview

Photo ☐ Yes / ☐ No

_____

_____

## Let the Journey Begin—Number of Correspondence

| ̶H̶I̶ II | Sent to contact | ̶H̶I̶ II | Received from contact |
|---|---|---|---|
| | E-mail messages | | E-mail messages |
| | Emoticons (winks, smiles, etc.) | | Emoticons (winks, smiles, etc.) |
| | Phone calls | | Phone calls |
| | Virtual dates initiated | | Virtual dates initiated |
| | Live dates initiated | | Live dates initiated |
| | U.S. mail | | U.S. mail |
| | Other | | Other |

## Miscellaneous

_____

_____

_____

# The Online Journey II

Initial thought of profile:

_____

Initial thought of correspondence:

_____

What I like most:

_____

What I like least:

_____

## Comments

Document key information that you want to remember.
*(i.e., great conversationalist, cried on first date, great voice, member looking for long-term relationship, etc.)*

_____
_____
_____
_____
_____
_____
_____
_____
_____
_____

## Blocked Member Details

Date: _____     Blocking Method: _____

Reasons/Details:

_____
_____
_____

# The Online Journey I

## Contact Data

Screen Name: _____    Legal Name: _____

Online Dating Service: _____    Date contact initiated: _____

☐ I initiated contact    ☐ He/She initiated contact

The reason I made contact or responded to contact:

_____

## Exchange of Personal Data

Date I sent personal data: _____    Date I received personal data: _____

Address: _____    City: _____    State: _____    Zip: _____

Age: _____    Height: _____    Other: _____

Contact Numbers:    Home: _____    Mobile: _____    Other: _____

E-mail address:

## Photo Overview

Photo ☐ Yes / ☐ No

_____

_____

## Let the Journey Begin—Number of Correspondence

| ЖＩＩ | Sent to contact | ЖＩＩ | Received from contact |
|---|---|---|---|
| | E-mail messages | | E-mail messages |
| | Emoticons (winks, smiles, etc.) | | Emoticons (winks, smiles, etc.) |
| | Phone calls | | Phone calls |
| | Virtual dates initiated | | Virtual dates initiated |
| | Live dates initiated | | Live dates initiated |
| | U.S. mail | | U.S. mail |
| | Other | | Other |

## Miscellaneous

_____

_____

_____

# The Online Journey II

Initial thought of profile:

_____

Initial thought of correspondence:

_____

What I like most:

_____

What I like least:

_____

## Comments

Document key information that you want to remember.
*(i.e., great conversationalist, cried on first date, great voice, member looking for long-term relationship, etc.)*

_____
_____
_____
_____
_____
_____
_____
_____
_____

## Blocked Member Details

Date: _____     Blocking Method: _____

Reasons/Details:

_____
_____
_____

# The Online Journey I

## Contact Data

Screen Name: _____    Legal Name: _____

Online Dating Service: _____    Date contact initiated: _____

☐ I initiated contact    ☐ He/She initiated contact

The reason I made contact or responded to contact:

_____

## Exchange of Personal Data

Date I sent personal data: _____    Date I received personal data: _____

Address: _____    City: _____ State: _____ Zip: _____

Age: _____    Height: _____    Other: _____

Contact Numbers:    Home: _____    Mobile: _____    Other: _____

E-mail address:

## Photo Overview

Photo ☐ Yes / ☐ No

_____
_____

## Let the Journey Begin—Number of Correspondence

| ⊮ II | Sent to contact | ⊮ II | Received from contact |
|---|---|---|---|
|  | E-mail messages |  | E-mail messages |
|  | Emoticons (winks, smiles, etc.) |  | Emoticons (winks, smiles, etc.) |
|  | Phone calls |  | Phone calls |
|  | Virtual dates initiated |  | Virtual dates initiated |
|  | Live dates initiated |  | Live dates initiated |
|  | U.S. mail |  | U.S. mail |
|  | Other |  | Other |

## Miscellaneous

_____
_____
_____

# The Online Journey II

Initial thought of profile:
_____

Initial thought of correspondence:
_____

What I like most:
_____

What I like least:
_____

## Comments

Document key information that you want to remember.
*(i.e., great conversationalist, cried on first date, great voice, member looking for long-term relationship, etc.)*

_____
_____
_____
_____
_____
_____
_____
_____
_____

## Blocked Member Details

Date: _____ Blocking Method: _____

Reasons/Details:
_____
_____
_____

*Know when to listen; know when to speak.*

# The Online Journey I

## Contact Data

Screen Name: _____    Legal Name: _____

Online Dating Service: _____    Date contact initiated: _____

☐ I initiated contact    ☐ He/She initiated contact

The reason I made contact or responded to contact:

_____

## Exchange of Personal Data

Date I sent personal data: _____    Date I received personal data: _____

Address: _____    City: _____ State: _____ Zip: _____

Age: _____    Height: _____    Other: _____

Contact Numbers:    Home: _____    Mobile: _____    Other: _____

E-mail address:

### Photo Overview

Photo ☐ Yes / ☐ No

_____

_____

## Let the Journey Begin—Number of Correspondence

| ~~IIII~~ II | Sent to contact | ~~IIII~~ II | Received from contact |
|---|---|---|---|
| | E-mail messages | | E-mail messages |
| | Emoticons (winks, smiles, etc.) | | Emoticons (winks, smiles, etc.) |
| | Phone calls | | Phone calls |
| | Virtual dates initiated | | Virtual dates initiated |
| | Live dates initiated | | Live dates initiated |
| | U.S. mail | | U.S. mail |
| | Other | | Other |

## Miscellaneous

_____

_____

_____

# The Online Journey II

**Member Rating:** 1 2 3 4 5 6 7 8 9 10 / ☺ ☺ ☹

Initial thought of profile:
_____

Initial thought of correspondence:
_____

What I like most:
_____

What I like least:
_____

## Comments
Document key information that you want to remember.
*(i.e., great conversationalist, cried on first date, great voice, member looking for long-term relationship, etc.)*

_____
_____
_____
_____
_____
_____
_____
_____
_____

## Blocked Member Details

Date: _____    Blocking Method: _____

Reasons/Details:
_____
_____
_____

# Safety First

Each online dating service offers a list of safety tips. It is to your advantage to read the tips and adhere to them. Please note that each online dating service posts disclaimers as well. The online dating services hold you responsible for your dating choices. Protecting your safety actually boils down to using common sense, listening to your instincts, and making smart decisions.

As an adult, you are ultimately accountable for making the right decisions in your life, so don't get so head over heels about a member that you can't see the forest for the sleaze. In other words, if a member seems desperate, then he or she probably is. If something doesn't feel right, then it probably isn't. The same safety measures that you use day-to-day are the same measures to use with online dating.

Become a part-time detective, and do some digging prior to meeting someone in person. Use an Internet search engine to find out more about your potential match. There are many search engines that can provide key information about your date.

Only meet when you are ready, and always meet in a safe place. Do not succumb to pressure from a member.

Always let someone else know the details of your date and when you are scheduled to return home. Have you read the headlines lately? Be safe.

Report any threats or attacks to the proper authorities.

<u>**Always ask yourself why, and be honest with your answers.**</u>

If a member is pressuring you to meet, ask yourself why. Move on.

If a member is being evasive, ask yourself why. Is he or she hiding something? Move on.

If a member asks a lot of personal financial questions, ask yourself why. Remember to protect your financial safety as well as your physical safety.

If you accept a date, ask yourself why. Do not accept a date just because you haven't been on one in six months. (Oops, that's my story.☺)

Minimize your risk by using your head, and always remember that your safety comes first.

If you see smoke, assume there's fire. You know what to do—stop, drop, and roll right out of there!

# Virtual Dates—Your Place *and Mine?*

*Creative virtual date ideas*

Congratulations! You have made several contacts, and you're on your way to growing fabulous relationships. Remember to take your time because love is patient. The e-mails and telephone conversations are great, and you want to take it to another level, but you're not quite ready for face-to-face action. This section contains online dating ideas that you can use with the help of technology and a good long-distance plan.

## Virtual Dating

Virtual date: An event between two individuals utilizing technology, creativity, and imagination.

Sometimes single folks do not feel comfortable going out to movies or to dinner alone, so the following ideas may be a stretch. Keep in mind that they have proven successful, especially with members in different locations and cities.

There are endless opportunities to add variety to your dating experiences without being in the same space or city. In the beginning, you may be a little apprehensive when using these techniques, but all you need is an open mind and a little imagination.

Virtual dinner date at home—The dinner should be planned just as with any other date. There should be a set date and time. The dinner should be prepared and on the table at the scheduled time.

- A speaker phone or headset should be used for ease and comfort.
- A Web cam is an awesome bonus!
- Do not multitask or watch TV while eating dinner. The focus should be on the date/event, just as if you were in a restaurant.
- Make it an elegant dinner with wine, salad, and dessert, or do a causal dinner. It's your choice.
- Do not pretend to have dinner just because you are not in the same room. Actually have dinner. You will be pleasantly surprised at the results.

Virtual date in the park—Simulate a park in your backyard or living room. Pull out the blankets or lawn chairs and a bottle of your favorite wine. Then, lay back and chat.

Virtual brunch on the patio—How do Sunday, mimosas, and a cool breeze sound?

Virtual happy hour—If possible, select the same restaurant in your respective locations and share an appetizer.

Be spontaneous; try text messaging—Take five to ten minutes to exchange text messages. It can be fun and inexpensive. Almost everyone has a mobile device, whether it's a cell phone or PDA. Use your imagination.

Shopping trip—Take him/her online shopping with you. This is a creative way to learn about style preferences or just another way to hear his/her voice. ☺

Virtual taste test—Create a shopping list of different types of natural foods or foods that do not need to be prepared *(e.g., fruits, veggies, creams, and sauces)*. Set a date and time. Prior to the taste test, display all of the food in a setting where you and your date can sample the same foods at the same time (in separate locations). This event will allow you and your date the time to actually describe the texture, taste, and scent of each food. The conversation will be directed toward how well you are in tune with your senses. The conversation is guaranteed to lead into many different topics. Yum, Yum!

# Virtual Dates—Your Place *and Mine?*

*Creative virtual date ideas*

## Virtual Dating

Name that song—Share your taste in music. Plan a Friday or Saturday evening to play music to each other. Yes, like when you were kids. Have some fun, and let your guard down—no one will know. Have a glass of wine, lay back, and enjoy. Try sampling music that is not commonly heard on the airwaves. This may take a bit of preplanning on your part, or not. Regardless, have fun.

Karaoke—How about a song and a smile? Why not sing together? It's guaranteed to bring a smile (or two) and laughter. Remember you don't have to be perfect.

A gift from the heart—Send images of flowers, gifts, or poetry prior to your virtual dates. This is great and inexpensive.

> *Tip: Don't worry about disturbing other patrons of the restaurant. Having a conversation over the phone is no different than talking to someone sitting in front of you. A word of advice, though, is to put your phone on silent or vibrate, and don't talk so loud as to disturb others.*

## Virtual Theme Dating

Movie theme—Plan to see the same movie, and then have a virtual date to discuss the theme, main characters, plot, and ending. Try reenacting the scenes. Don't be embarrassed; let loose and have some fun! Keep the date focused on the movie.

Sports fan(tastic) date—World Series, Final Four, Wimbledon, Super Bowl. What's your pleasure? There's something for everyone. Plan a sporting event that you can watch together, play-by-play, blow-by-blow. It's more fun than you could ever imagine.

Dream vacations—Plan a virtual dream vacation (i.e., share destinations and reasons for the choices until you both agree on the same destination). Plan the meals, the duration, and the events. The conversation will allow you to learn about each other's desires. Make your own rules.

> *Tip: Keep notes; you may need this information for a major event in the future. (Wink, wink.)*

# Virtual Dates—Your Place *and Mine?*

Document your own virtual date ideas.
Log on to www.theonlinedatingjournal.us to share your virtual date ideas.

# The Online Dating Experience
*Advice from the Author*

As you indulge in the world of online dating, consciously take the time to clear your mind of day-to-day pressures. Your online dating experiences should be pleasurable. Begin with a positive attitude, and your rewards will be plentiful.

*The Online Dating Journal* provides you with the guidance you will need as you venture into the online dating community. Remember to scan the globe, get in your comfort zone, block when you have to, and, most of all, enjoy. As you find matches and begin to correspond, use your imagination and be creative. Take the time to indulge in virtual dating; it provides a safe environment to learn more about your potential matches.

There are numerous ways to make online dating enjoyable, and *The Online Dating Journal* provides you with the basic principles of online dating.

If you are not attracting quality, compatible matches, you may want to expand your horizons. If initially you were not open to long-distance relationships, you may want to reevaluate the pros and cons of it. One of the pros of a long-distance relationship is companionship with personal space. (Yeah, baby!) Long-distance relationships also help you improve your communication skills and your ability to trust. Try it. You will be pleasantly surprised at what is happening outside of your local circle.

Your success with online dating is highly dependent on your level of honesty and confidence. There is no need for lies. Fabricating aspects of your life will ultimately destroy the trust in your relationship. Any relationship without trust as the foundation will eventually crumble. The truth is so much easier to remember than a lie, wouldn't you agree?

If you're attracting the undesirable "oh my" men or women, you may want to review and update your profile. We all could use a nip and tuck here and there, and a minor makeover will freshen your profile, giving it some curb appeal. Need help? Check out your online dating service Web site. Most Web sites offer tips on how to gain the most from your dating experience. They also provide specific tips on profile enhancements.

As you scan the globe, keep an open mind. Although safety is of the utmost concern, do not be overly suspicious and inadvertently rule out your knight in shining armor. Remember not everyone is photogenic. Try to look beyond the physical appearances.

I was advised once to change my potential match settings to encompass a larger region. As a result, my number of compatible suitors increased. I have met the most interesting people and learned about different cultures, and these encounters have enriched my life tremendously. In fact, I have met a true gentleman, and we have been corresponding for over a year. No, he's not my soul mate, but he is the yummiest friend I could ever ask for. We have vowed to be online friends for life.

Please take great pleasure in using *The Online Dating Journal*, as it is focused on the specific needs of the online dater. Make memories of each experience. It's your life. Live it to the fullest, and have no regrets. Here's wishing you much success!

# Notes

# Notes

# Notes

# Notes

# Notes

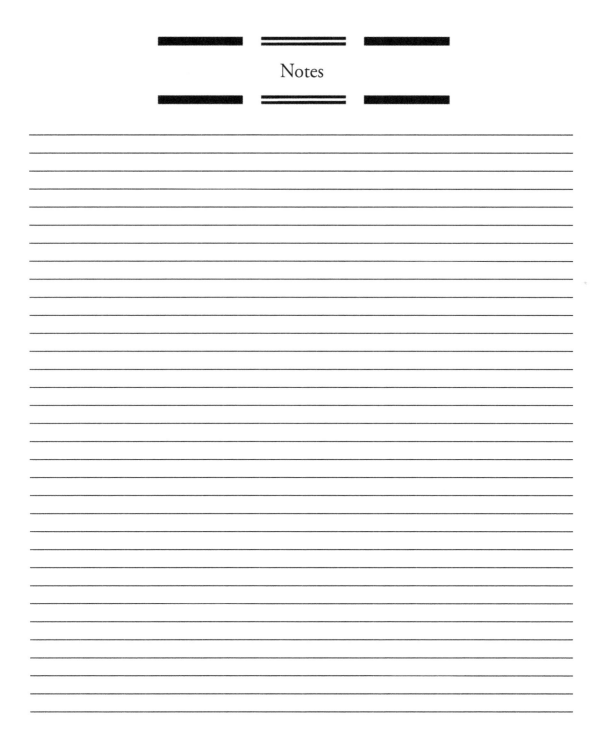

# Notes

# Notes

# Notes

# Notes

# Notes

# Notes

# Personal Acknowledgments

Throughout life there will be people who touch you in ways that words cannot express. These are the people who, when you think of the experiences that you share, cause tears uncontrollably to fill your eyes. It's love, in its truest form.

These are my tears.

To my sister, Grace Bergeron, my biggest cheerleader. Thank you for listening to concept after concept after concept. You were the one person who would honestly tell me that I was over the top and needed to come back. Thank you for collaborating and for your loyalty to this project. To John and J. R. Bergeron, the world's best brother-in-law and nephew a chick could ask for. A sincere thank-you for your generosity and for feeding me on the holidays (and yes, I prayed for you).

To my brothers, James C. Miller and John H. Miller Jr. These two men substantiate the phrase, "Blood is thicker than water." There is nothing we wouldn't do for each other. Thank you for providing love and security. I love you and miss you very much. Remember, I am only a few hours away.

To my extended family members, Sylvia Kendrick and Yvette and Tony Brown. Your encouragement and support over the past twenty-five years have enriched my life tremendously. *Can you believe that it has been twenty-five years?* Your personal achievements have been an inspiration for me in many ways. Thank you for believing in my abilities and for just being there. Thank you for the love.

When I look over my life, it seems that about every ten years or so I have been blessed with the gift of friendship. I send love and gratitude to Horace Jordan, Eric Shepherd, L. Kathy Morrow, and E. Melody Watkins. You are my mentors, my confidants. You make me laugh until it hurts. Your friendship keeps me balanced and adds immeasurable value to my life. Thank you for your words of wisdom and encouragement throughout the years. It is a privilege to call you my friends.

Diahana Cousar, my very first friend—Happy birthday! Now I'm covered for life.

To all of my friends, thank you for the collaboration, the laughter, and for listening to my crazy stories. I am glad that we met.

A sincere thank-you to the readers for purchasing *The Online Dating Journal.* I hope that this journal provides you with much success with your online dating experiences.

~ Anita

978-0-595-36543-2
0-595-36543-4

www.ingramcontent.com/pod-product-compliance
Lightning Source LLC
Chambersburg PA
CBHW080355060326
40689CB00019B/4016